I Believe in Evangelism

By the same author:

TOWARDS TOMORROW'S CHURCH

MY GOD IS REAL

GOD'S FREEDOM FIGHTERS

ONE IN THE SPIRIT

IN SEARCH OF GOD

LIVE A NEW LIFE

I Believe in Evangelism

by

DAVID WATSON

WILLIAM B. EERDMANS PUBLISHING COMPANY

Library of Congress Cataloging in Publication Data
Watson, David C   K   1933-
    I believe in evangelism.

    1.   Evangelistic work.   I.   Title.
BV3790.W327   1977   269'.2   77-2229
ISBN 0-8028-1687-8

To John Collins who showed me the
way to Christ, and who helped me
to bring Christ to others.

Acknowledgments

I want to acknowledge my debt to a number of people who have helped me with this manuscript: to the Revd. John Brook, Chaplain of Massey University, New Zealand, for stimulating my thoughts and for researching into some material for chapters two and three especially; to Paul Burbridge for his careful reading of the manuscript; and to Mary Pratt, Sue Hope and Judy Frampton for their patient typing. Also, I am especially grateful to Canon Michael Green and Canon Max Warren for their generous encouragement, and for their illuminating comments which have been incorporated into the book.

Biblical quotations, unless otherwise stated, are from the Revised Standard Version.

Contents

Editor's Preface

EVANGELISM IS STILL in many quarters of the church considered a dirty word. It has the sniff of proselytising about it, of big meetings and famous but perhaps simplistic and slick preachers. It is suggestive of illicit psychological pressure, and if it has a particularly notable impact, of mass hysteria. And yet...does not evangelism mean the spreading of good news? And if you have found good news, it is churlish indeed to keep it to yourself. If you are thrilled about it, why should you not show it? If you see the need others have of it, then you are likely to give yourself to enabling them to discover it.

Evangelism is basically a matter of truth. Is it true that there is but one God, and he a God of perfect holiness and perfect love? Is it true that he has come to our world in the person of Jesus of Nazareth to show us what he is like, and to reconcile us from our alienation into his family? Is it true that the living God can come and indwell a man's life, and transform him utterly? If it is, then it is not only permissible for a Christian to spread such good news; it is incumbent upon him.

It is from this position of discovery and confidence in the power of the good news that David Watson writes. Moreover, he writes from a position of great experience. After a baptism of fire in the dockland parish of Gillingham where he served a distinguished curacy, followed by a spell in as different a milieu as you could imagine, among the undergraduates at Cambridge, he went to York and was entrusted with overseeing the funeral rites, so to speak, of an inner city church that was about to close through disuse. Beginning with a tiny handful, he saw the power of the gospel change the lives of countless ordinary citizens of York. His church was soon packed; it was linked up to other halls by closed-circuit T.V.; and before long he was given charge of a much larger church (also on the verge of closure) right opposite York Minster. It is now thronged with people. Do not get the impression that the church is perfect: it bristles with problems. It is, nevertheless a remarkable church, and it does not depend on David Watson for its impact. Indeed, if you ask him, he will tell you that it tends to grow more when he is away on an evangelistic tour in some other part of the world than when he is there at the helm! Why? Because he actually carries out the principles of delegation, trust, training and oversight to which many church leaders give lip service. He has solved the problem of financing workers in the church. It is simple. Get Christians to live together in households where, say, half the members go out to work, and support the other half who are thereby freed to work full time in the congregation in a thousand and one ways — visiting, care of the sick and the mentally handicapped, running Christian shops, making music and dance and drama, and so on.

It will be apparent by now that David Watson is well equipped to write about evangelism, which he devotes himself to through public preaching and personal conversations, in universities throughout the world, in city-wide campaigns and in schools. But it should also be apparent that his perspective is very different from the traditional brand image of evangelism. He operates no one man band, no mindless frenzy of decision-making, no emotional challenge. People are coming to the faith spontaneously and at times daily in his congregation, not only because of the preaching, but because of the impact of the whole congregation, the quality of its worship, the changes in men's lives, the prayers of that mid-week meeting for praise and intercession which brings some two hundred of the congregation together to beseech God's blessing.

This is, I fancy, the most important book David Watson has yet written. It enshrines principles of evangelism that I have never seen in print before. It is rooted in experience. It is grounded in a remarkable grasp of the New Testament. It is alive with the freshness and power of the Holy Spirit. It will have a very great impact in inspiring congregational-based, worshipful evangelism in many parts of the world. I commend it to you...and your friends.

Michael Green

CHAPTER ONE

The Moods and Questions of Today

THE URGENCY OF EVANGELISM

TODAY THERE IS one theme that is being discussed by Christians throughout the world. It calls for greater urgency than the issues raised by the 'charismatic' or ecumenical movements. It inescapably involves every true Christian, regardless of denomination, churchmanship or theological persuasion. It concerns a clear command given to the Church by Christ: his last command before his ascension into heaven, and of such importance that it is recorded in all four Gospels and in the Acts of the Apostles. It is the foremost task of the Church, next to worship, and there has never been a time in the history of the world when the need to take this task seriously has been so imperative. It is, of course, the task of evangelism. As someone has expressed it, 'Compared with evangelism, everything else happening in the church is like re-arranging the furniture when the house is on fire.'

A series of sobering facts should make us sit up and think. First of all, we are faced with *the awe-inspiring needs of the world.* Statistics can often become meaningless. But it is worth remembering, as you read this, that within the next hour some 4-500 in the world will die from starvation, and a further 6,000 will die from other causes. At the same time more than 14,000 babies will be born. This means that, according to the present rate of explosion, the world popula-tion *increases* by approximately 8,000 every hour or 200,000 every day, the majority of whom will be born into areas where there is little or no knowledge of Christ. Although there are 1,000 million professing Christians in the world, this leaves some 2,000 million who are not. Or, to emphasise the size of the task confronting the Church, there are twice as many non-Christians in the world today as at the turn of the century. Moreover, by the turn of the next century the world population will have doubled!

Secondly, we are confronted in some countries, such as Britain, with *a steady drop in church membership* year by year. Although we can be encouraged by the remarkable growth of Christian churches in parts of Latin America or Korea, Europe is less than 5 per cent Christian; and in the vast continent of Asia, which contains more than one half of the world's population, at least 95 per cent are avowedly non-Christian. In Britain, the story is too often told of dwindling congregations and redundant church buildings, and although there are some thrilling signs of the Spirit's renewal, the popular image of the Church is pathetic and depressing. The *Weekend Telegraph* summed up the secular view of the Church with scornful pity: 'The Anglican priests of England, a motley band of underpaid and generally frustrated men, provide some of the most poignant casualties of the twentieth century. They suffer nervous breakdowns through lack of money, waste hours trudging the countryside, peddling faith to the sceptical, and reap untold depressions by preaching in ill-repaired churches to diminishing and elderly congregations.' As in all caricatures, there is uncomfortably more than a grain of truth in this tragi-comedy. Far too many ministers and clergy are questioning their whole *raison d'être*: they have lost confidence as heralds of Christ. The drop-out rate is increasing. Correspondingly there is a marked growth in the religious cults of today: Mormonism, Occultism, Jehovah's Witnesses, Divine Light Mission — not to mention the phenomenal progress of Communism over the last fifty years. All these movements are in part a rebuke to the apathy of the Christian Church, and they are sharp reminders of power and dedicated discipleship. A Communist once threw out this challenge to a Christian:

The gospel is a much more powerful weapon for the renewal of society than is our Marxist philosophy, but all the same it is we who will finally beat *you*... We communists do not play with words. We are realists, and seeing that we are determined to achieve our object, we know how to obtain the means. Of our salaries and wages we keep only what is strictly necessary, and we give up our free time and part of our holidays. You, however, give only a little time and hardly any money for the spreading of the gospel of Christ. How can anybody believe in the supreme value of this gospel if you do not practise it, if you do not spread it, and if you sacrifice neither time nor money for it...? We believe in our Communist message and we are ready to sacrifice everything, even our life... But you people are afraid even to soil your hands.

Until we Christians take seriously the instructions of our Master by denying ourselves, taking up our cross and following him, we have nothing to say in reply to that challenge.

I once heard Brother Andrew speak of a time when he was sitting with another Christian in a bus in Vietnam. They saw a man carrying a basket walking in front of the bus. It was during the time of intensive fighting and constant Vietcong guerrilla attacks.

'Watch out!' said the Christian. 'In that basket there might well be a bomb!'

'Why are you so afraid?' asked Brother Andrew.

'That man may be a Vietcong who will throw himself and the basket at the bus,' came the reply. 'He doesn't mind if he dies. I do!'

Brother Andrew commented on this incident, 'That sums up the ineffectiveness of so much of the Church today!' How many Christians are willing to lay down their lives for Jesus Christ? Certainly many have done so. In this century alone there have probably been more Christian martyrs than in the entire history of the Christian Church put together. Hundreds of thousands have died for their faith in the Congo, Kenya, Burundi, Papua, Ecuador, China, Russia, Romania, and many other countries. However, in places where persecution today is not so violent, the spirit of self-sacrifice is not always so obvious. How many are willing to lay down their

worldly ambitions, their money and possessions, their privacy
and privileges, their selfish desires, their comforts and securities? With the greatest urgency we need to recapture the spirit
of Paul who wrote, 'I look upon everything as loss compared
with the overwhelming gain of knowing Christ Jesus my
Lord';[1] or of David Livingstone who said, 'I place no value on
anything, except in its relation to the Kingdom of God.'
Certainly the task of evangelism is urgent in the gathering
gloom and despair of today's world.

THE MOODS AND QUESTIONS OF TODAY

It is not enough for the gospel to *be* relevant (as every true
Christian will believe); it must be *seen* to be relevant before
there can be any effective communication. William Temple
once caricatured theologians as 'men who spend blameless
lives giving entirely orthodox answers to questions no-one is
asking'. When today's generation dismisses the Church for
being remote and irrelevant, we cannot ignore what Temple
was trying to say. Christ has entrusted us with the ministry of
reconciliation, and this demands keeping very closely in
touch both with the world and with God. Jesus not only
spoke with great authority, which astonished his hearers; he
was also utterly relevant to the daily needs of ordinary people,
which is why, initially at least, he was so popular with the
'tax collectors and sinners' who were ostracised by the
hypocritical piety of the religious leaders. His message got
through: it was powerful communication. So what are the
moods and questions of today?

Perhaps most of all we need to concentrate on the moods,
because whilst the moods are deeply felt, explicit questions
which pinpoint the frustrations of today are not always being
asked. This is the age of the 'hidden persuaders': society as a
whole is being profoundly influenced, in an almost entirely
subliminal or subconscious way, by values and philosophies of
life which can radically change people and nations in a
remarkably short space of time. It is significant that most
revolutions have been sparked into life by a tiny group of
highly intelligent men studying carefully, and giving expression to, the moods of the working and oppressed classes. The

philosophy of Nietsche influenced Hitler and the Nazi movement; Marx and Lenin brought into being the Communist revolution, which has swallowed up a third of the world in sixty years. The *Thoughts* of Mao tse Tung have changed the face of the East beyond all recognition in thirty years. Likewise the writings of Jean-Paul Sartre, Herbert Marcuse and others have influenced the thinking of those in the West more than many realise. It is also significant that the spiritual revolution of the Christian Church has usually followed a similar pattern. Granted the sovereign power of the Spirit of God, there have nearly always been able and thinking leaders who have rightly understood the moods of the people. We have Paul in the first century unfolding the truths and relevance of the gospel for Jews and Gentiles alike. We have Luther, Calvin, Tyndale, Latimer, and Cranmer at the time of the Reformation. We have Wesley and Whitefield in the eighteenth century, who, although men of considerable academic ability, were able to relate to the ordinary working folk, totally disenchanted as they were by the established religion of the day. We have Shaftesbury, Wilberforce, Booth, Hannah More and Josephine Butler in the nineteenth century, who saw the foolishness of preaching words to people when they were still trapped by slavery or the evils of the Industrial Revolution. Here were men who were passionately concerned with the immediate relevance of the gospel for their own generation, refusing to be shackled by the churchy traditions of the past, and being willing to break out into fresh ground, whilst remaining true to God's revelation in the Scriptures. This is what the Church *must* do today. It must understand, and seek to meet, the real needs of real people, or else it will soon become moribund and fossilised — a popular image that, tragically, is associated with the Church at this present time.

There can be little doubt that the prevalent mood of today is *apathy*. 'Why bother? Who cares? Don't get involved!' These are the slogans of the modern world. Kitty Genovese, aged twenty-eight, was trailed by a man in Kew Gardens, New York, in March 1964. He attacked and killed her. At least forty people heard her scream and shout for help, and many of them must have seen her die. Yet no one came to her rescue or even called for the police. 'I didn't want to get involved,' explained one of the eye-witnesses. In Toledo, Ohio, in 1965 a truck-driver rushed over to an overturned car which had caught fire, and dragged the trapped woman driver away from certain death. 'Whadda yer want to do that for?' asked an irritated bystander who had obviously felt cheated of witnessing a gruesome fatality which might have coloured, for a day at least, his otherwise colourless existence. Indeed, the paralysis of apathy can often be the prelude to *violence*, because behind both apathy and violence is deeply-rooted frustration. For some it may be the intractable problems of pollution, over-population or the nuclear arms-race. No matter how often the experts issue warning after warning, and forecast disaster after disaster, these awe-inspiring problems continue to roll towards us, like enormous snowballs, with ever-increasing size and speed. Problems are endlessly analysed, and their consequences, spelt out on the media with alarming clarity, produce both fear and frustration in society, with no hope of finding any realistic solutions. The problems become clearer, but the answers more remote.

For others, the unspoken fear is the increasing depersonalisation of the individual in our urban, technological society. There is also a striking correlation between violence and social deprivation; and if, as Leslie Paul suggests, 'that sense of deprivation is made greater and more compelling by the anonymity and humiliation of crowded, complex, rundown city areas, then the probability is that violence will increase as cities grow…in the population explosion which seems upon us.'[2] Certainly, the greater the sense of hopelessness and helplessness, the greater the inner rage (often suppressed in the early stages by apathy or depression) and the stronger the readiness to strike out, or to strike back. John Paul Scott has shown, in *The Anatomy of Violence*, that the incidence of violence is almost perfectly correlated with the size of the city, because it is so often in the large city that personal insignificance, loneliness, boredom and alienation are most keenly felt.

We need, therefore, to look a little more closely at the root causes of the apathy and violence which characterise so much of today's world. Inevitably we must start with the penetrating analysis that Christ gave: that the heart of the human problem is the problem of the human heart. Ultimately, all the evils of society can be traced back to the inherent *selfishness* of man's fallen nature. 'For from within, out of the heart of man, come evil thoughts, fornication, theft, murder, adultery, coveting, wickedness, deceit, licentiousness, envy, slander, pride, foolishness.'[3] Read the second half of Romans 1, where Paul describes what happens when man turns his back on the truth about God that can be known: it reads like the front page of one of the seamier Sunday newspapers. Elsewhere he spells out the 'works of the flesh', or our natural self-life, in these terms: 'impure thoughts, eagerness for lustful pleasure, idolatry, spiritism, hatred and fighting, jealousy and anger, constant effort to get the best for yourself, complaints and criticisms, the feeling that everyone else is wrong except those in your own little group...envy, murder, drunkenness, wild parties, and all that sort of thing'.[4] Once we accept the biblical view of man, we should cease to be surprised by the covetousness which dominates our society today; by the endless strikes for higher wages, regardless of the crippling effect this has on the national economy; by the constant pursuit of money and possessions, even when this denies human values and destroys personal relationships. Politicians promise monotonously to 'raise the standard of living', but the implicit assumption is that 'living' is synonymous with 'earning'. It is what *I* get out of it, in terms of hard cash, that determines the value of many a job. It is still pungently true that 'those who desire to be rich fall into temptation, into a snare, into many senseless and hurtful desires that plunge men into ruin and destruction. For the love of money is the root of all evils.'[5] Every now and then, of course, the materialist's dream comes true. How many viewers would love to be in television's *Generation Game,* sitting in that prized seat at the end of the programme watching twenty or more luxury items pass by, all of which can be yours if you remember them within forty-five seconds? There are a sufficient number of fulfilled dreams to encourage the materialist to go on dreaming, the gambler to go on gambling, the father to go on filling in those pools coupons. Money is seen to be the ultimate in self-fulfilment. Certainly, any analysis of today's moods which does not focus on the basic selfishness and covetousness of man misses the heart of it all.

However, it is a simplistic view of our evangelistic task to say that if the heart of the individual is changed, all problems will be solved. It is not so easy as that. For example, the natural self-centredness of man is made more acute today by the widespread *breakdown of communication* at all levels. There is little or no community life, especially in urban areas; there is little job satisfaction in the increasingly complex scientific and industrial society in which we live. Most people are right in that they are little more than tiny cogs in a vast impersonal machine. Some even lack the cold comfort of feeling that they are cogs at all. In his arresting book *The Greening of America*, Charles Reich wrote:

> The immense apparatus of technology and organization that America has built…has become a mindless juggernaut, destroying the environment, obliterating human values, and assuming domination over the lives and minds of its subjects. To the injustices and exploitation of the nineteenth century the Corporate State has added depersonalization, meaninglessness and repression, until it has threatened to destroy all meaning and all life.[6]

The creative skill of the craftsman, who has the satisfaction of seeing the job from start to finish, is largely a thing of the past. Work has become little more than a necessary evil, in order to buy expensive toys and clothes for the kids, fitted carpets for the home, a second car for the wife, and a coloured telly to keep everyone entertained without the effort of having to make conversation or to create relationships. Sociologists have suggested several reasons for the breakdown of marriages:

(1) Mobility. One out of three families in which the husband is under thirty-five moves each year. This tends to breed insecurity and instability.

(2) The depersonalisation of human beings in our computerised society. The resultant loneliness, aimlessness,

frustration, despair and self-pity are certainly not conducive to successful marriages.

(3) The sexual revolution. Premarital and extramarital affairs are among the most deadly and destructive forces attacking marriage today.

(4) Affluence. Our materialistic culture practically eliminates the meaningful interpersonal relationships necessary for a happy home.

(5) Growing permissiveness in training children. We are producing an undisciplined generation of young people who are poorly equipped to establish successful homes.

(6) Radio and TV. Their shallow portrayal of love and their addictive tyranny of time make an effective home life most difficult.[7]

Naturally this failure in communication leads to *boredom*. This is a spectator generation. It is so easy to give the kids instant amusement with a click on the telly, and so much harder to think up creative and imaginative games or hobbies, which could involve several members of the household. No doubt one reason for the outstanding success, on both sides of the Atlantic, of such television serials as *The Forsyte Saga* and *The Pallisers* is that these stories speak of an age of comparative stability and of meaningful human relationships; an age where family life and fortune is of the essence; where there is time, space and inclination to follow up every minor alley-way, every slightest thread, to its conclusion, and to see the whole pattern satisfyingly complete at the end. By contrast, life today is fast, bewildering, incomplete; few issues find their conclusion, and fewer still 'live happily ever after' outside the fantasy world of a television serial. Instead there are pressures causing neuroses of epidemic proportions. Television is a momentary escape, yet an escape which has begun to cripple communication between people, in both the home and the neighbourhood. The individual becomes increasingly lost in himself. The world becomes increasingly *my* world, where my interests and my concerns are the only ones worth bothering about.

Trapped in our own separate little boxes, it is hardly surprising that one of the greatest social problems of today is *loneliness.* There is a desperate need to belong to an open, loving and accepting group, and yet there is all the fear of personal inadequacy when it comes to being involved. Further, the huge concentration by the media on youth, beauty, fashion, and sexual attraction makes more acute than ever the isolation of those who feel disqualified in any or all of these areas. Redundancy, or even the threat of it, increases the sense of rejection and futility. 'I can't see any point in living' is a remark I hear too often for it to be dismissed lightheartedly. One girl, who had attempted suicide on twelve occasions, told me that she was afraid to live and she was afraid to die.

In this atmosphere of almost complete frustration, *self-pity* and *self-hatred* breed like maggots. The protests today, the verbal or physical violence, the criticisms and judgments made about one another are frequently projections of our own self-hatred. To live consciously with this tormenting self-condemnation would prove to be unbearable; therefore we project the hatred on to someone or something else. This deep-seated bitterness in the hearts of individuals and groups of people is cancerous and destructive. It appears with horrifying force and senseless devastation in Northern Ireland and in the numerous liberation groups which are dedicated to kidnapping, hi-jacking, maiming and killing, sometimes with random futility. A psychiatrist working with these extremists commented that he found them hating themselves as much as they hated the objects of their violence; this self-hatred they could project in virtually any direction. Further, below the surface of vast numbers of decent and respectable citizens, with whom the idea of physical violence is anathema, there are often keenly-felt personal grievances, long-standing resentments, resulting in verbal violence and bad relationships, but frequently stemming at heart from a considerable degree of self-hatred. Here, the feeling of alienation can be almost overwhelming: we have forgotten how to live with others, and we cannot bear to live with ourselves.

Not surprisingly, many suffer today from bad consciences and feelings of *guilt.* This is particularly apparent when counselling those who are recently bereaved: there is an instinctive tendency to extol the virtues of the deceased and to justify the way in which he or she was treated throughout their lifetime — 'I did everything I could for him.' It is one thing for the philosophers to say that 'absolutes are out' and that there are no rights or wrongs — everything is relative, but it is quite another thing to silence that God-given part of us, which we call conscience. Thus many people today are both confused and guilty.

Existentialist philosophy has so infiltrated the fibre of society that, from almost every direction, the impression is given that whatever is possible in terms of personal experience is also justifiable. There is a brazen display of what used to be called immorality, homosexuality, pornography, dishonesty or deceit. At the same time it is impossible to eliminate the pricks of conscience, even if these become less painful by being constantly ignored. One way to escape from the pain and confusion is to become even more judgmental about the behaviour of others. When you throw a stone into a pack of dogs, the one that yelps loudest is the one that has been hit! I have often noticed that those who seek to justify their actions by claiming that absolutes are out are also those who shout most loudly that the behaviour of certain individuals, or certain sections of society, is absolutely wrong! Perhaps they yelp most loudly along these lines because their consciences are so often being hit! Once again, it is a question of projecting our guilt on to other people. How right Christ was when he told us to attend to the log that is in our own eye, before we could see clearly to take the speck out of another person's eye.

Coupled with these other moods, there is, unquestionably, a _spiritual hunger_: a hunger for God or for some kind of spiritual reality or power, something that is greater than ourselves, that will lift us out of ourselves into all that is meaningful and relevant in terms of personal experience. We can see this in the dramatic rise in occultism over the last decade: ouija boards, tarot cards, fortune-telling, horoscopes, astrology, white magic, black magic, witchcraft. The proliferation of expensive books on such pursuits indicates the public demand and its craving for spiritual experience. In August 1975 the World Congress of Witchcraft was held in Bogota,

Colombia, with 3,000 witches, sorcerers and spiritists attending. (There were approximately the same number of Christian workers at the 1974 Congress on World Evangelisation in Lausanne.) Workshops were held on astrology, palmistry, exorcism, voodoo and supernatural healing. However, whether or not people dabble in the occult, there is a growing desire for a 'one-world' religion. One secular example of this is the fanatical devotion to football which has, in many countries, become the religion of the people, complete with chanting, the worship of teams or players, costly dedication, and (amongst some) the ritual of violence. Another example, in the context of religious beliefs, is today's growing mood of toleration which encourages a syncretistic religion, in which all sharp edges are blurred and the unique and exclusive claims of Christianity are out. Largely because the Church has so often failed to speak with the clear authority of Scripture, most people are swayed by 'what the experts say', gathered from the superficial religious debates on television and from the Sunday newspapers, which, like the Athenians of old, try to spend their time in nothing but telling something 'new'. The trouble is that there is a very short step from believing in everything to believing in nothing. If everything is true, nothing is true. If every religious approach is equally valid, there is no objective validity or reality to be found. Everything is subjective, and subjectivism is but a step away from atheism. The search for a true spirituality, therefore, so often ends in further disillusionment and despair.

Out in the cold I stand,
Looking on at the world sitting tight,
With its people in their nice little worlds,
And the friends who don't even know me.
It makes no difference to their world where I am.
If I'm there, it keeps going.
If I'm not, it goes on.
While I walk around, wandering, wondering,
My mind a mass of mixed-up machinery,
Clashing with conflicts and unanswered questions.
I don't ask if the world is real —

It sits up there on its foundations,
Secure, concrete, hard and stone and real.
But I'm not real —
Or if I am, maybe I shouldn't be.
They answer, 'Smile, God loves you',
But I can't smile.
I'm numbed by cold inside and out.
Even the heat in the square brick buildings
Would only warm my body, nothing else.
I'm alone in a world full of people,
Apart, shut up inside myself,
Cold, unfeeling, in a cold unfeeling world.[8]

It could be argued, of course, that there is nothing significantly new about man today. Much the same frustrations were there in New Testament times, or even when Ecclesiastes was written. Although some of the immediate causes are naturally different in this technological age, the resultant moods are remarkably similar: apathy, violence, selfishness, broken relationships, boredom, loneliness, self-pity, self-hatred, guilt and spiritual hunger. However, a clear understanding of these moods, and the reasons for them, is of the greatest importance when it comes to evangelism. If our gospel does not speak to the *felt* needs of men and women today, it will not speak to them at all. Moreover, God's communication of himself to man is rich in variety, and always relevant. In our preaching and teaching, for example, we must be diligent in our study, not only of the Bible but also of the newspapers and of the cries of those around us. As we seek to build up a loving and united church, we should examine the practical ways in which broken relationships can be healed, and lonely people find unjudging friendship within the family of God. Perhaps it will be through signs and wonders, or through praise and prayer, that the apathy will be broken and questions will begin to be asked. Maybe there will have to be some prayerful re-organisation within the church if there is to be meaningful social action and service. What are the frustrations of the neighbourhood? How can Christians serve those outside the Kingdom of God in ways that will demonstrate his loving concern for all people, whether or not they acknowledge his name? In every church it will be invaluable for the leaders to consider carefully what, in their particular situation, it really means 'fully to preach the gospel of Christ ... by word and deed, by the power of signs and wonders, and by the power of the Holy Spirit'.[9] Clinging to the traditional patterns of the past will frequently result in wasted money and energy, with Christians preaching to Christians. What was relevant yesterday may be quite irrelevant today. Although the essential gospel never changes, the manner in which it is proclaimed and demonstrated must reveal the fact that we are dealing with the God of today. It is only when people hear his voice *today* that we can urge them, in the name of Christ, not to harden their hearts but to turn to him in true repentance and faith.

NOTES

1   Philippians 3:8 (J. B. Phillips), p.14.
2   'The Vogue of Violence', in *Christianity and Change*, ed. Autton (S.P.C.K.), 36, p.16.
3   Mark 7:21f, p.17.
4   Galatians 5:19-21 (*Living Bible*), p.17.
5   1 Timothy 6:9f, p.17.
6   Op. cit., 23, p.18.
7   R. L. Strauss, *Marriage is for love* (Tyndale), 10, p.18.
8   Found scribbled on an ink blotter on an empty desk, Fisher Hall, Wheaton College. Author unknown, p, 22.
9   Romans 15:18f, p. 24.

CHAPTER TWO

What is Evangelism?

NUMEROUS DEFINITIONS HAVE been suggested in the last half-century. Most famous, perhaps, is the one given by the Archbishops' Committee in 1918, in its report on the evangelistic work of the Church: 'To evangelize is so to present Christ Jesus in the power of the Holy Spirit, that men shall come to put their trust in God through him, to accept him as their Saviour, and serve him as their King in the fellowship of his Church.'[1]

Some have criticised certain details of this definition. Evangelism, they say, should not be defined in terms of the *effect* achieved in the lives of others; rather the essence of New Testament evangelism is simply in *proclaiming* the gospel. Dr. J. I. Packer, for example, suggested a redrafting of the 1918 definition in these words: 'To evangelize is to present Christ Jesus to sinful men in order that, through the power of the Holy Spirit, they *may* come to put their trust in God through him.'[2]

More recently the 1974 International Congress on World Evangelisation in Lausanne stated the meaning of evangelism in these terms:

> To evangelize is to spread the good news that Jesus Christ died for our sins and was raised from the dead according to the Scriptures, and that as the reigning Lord he now offers the forgiveness of sins and the liberating gift of the Spirit to all who repent and believe. Our Christian presence in the world is indispensable to evangelism, and so is that kind of

dialogue whose purpose is to listen sensitively in order to understand. But evangelism itself is the proclamation of the historical, biblical Christ as Saviour and Lord, with a view to persuading people to come to him personally and so be reconciled to God. In issuing the gospel invitation we have no liberty to conceal the cost of discipleship. Jesus still calls all who would follow him to deny themselves, take up their cross, and identify themselves with his new community. The results of evangelism include obedience to Christ, incorporation into his church and responsible service in the world.[3]

Similarly, the Report of the Evangelical Alliance Commission on Evangelism stressed the priority of the spoken word: 'The verb from which we derive the word *evangelism* is used in the New Testament to denote the spoken announcement of the Gospel with a view to the divine regeneration of the hearers... The word *evangelism* should therefore be restricted in meaning to announcing the message of salvation.'[4]

Our starting-point should, of course, be the New Testament itself, and therefore we need to examine a number of biblical words to understand the true nature of evangelism. Two groups of words need to be examined, the 'evangelism' and the 'proclamation' groups.

1. EVANGELISM

To evangelise

The verb *(euaggelizesthai)* is used fifty-two times in the New Testament, including twenty-five by Luke and twenty-one by Paul. Quite simply, 'to evangelise' means to announce or proclaim or bring good news. In the Septuagint of the Old Testament it is used sometimes of a runner coming with the news of victory; in the Psalms it occurs twice[5] in the sense of proclaiming God's faithfulness and salvation.

However, in the New Testament it is worth noting carefully that the word is frequently used in a rich context. For example, in Luke 4:18f. Jesus is reading from Isaiah, Chapter 61, during his customary visit to the Nazareth synagogue on the sabbath day: 'The Spirit of the Lord is upon me, because he has anointed me to preach good news *(euaggelisasthai)* to the poor. He has sent me to proclaim release to the captives and recovery of sight to the blind, to set at liberty those who are oppressed, to proclaim the acceptable year of the Lord.' Here we see at once that the proclamation of good news was linked directly with a *demonstration* of that good news. Jesus was sent by his Father to this world not merely to conduct a preaching tour, but to show the reality of the living God in a way that powerfully met the personal needs of people. Thus although the verb 'to evangelise', when strictly translated, means no more than to announce good news, it is unthinkable in the ministry of Jesus to separate the active verb from the action in which it is set.

Indeed, had this not been so, then the words of Jesus would have been empty words, typical of the vain boast of the false prophet. Therefore when John the Baptist was languishing in Herod's prison, waiting for his inevitable execution, it seemed to him that the 'good news' of Jesus had after all been in word only. Where was the evidence of its truth? 'Are you he who is to come?' he was asked by a messenger, 'or shall we look for another?' How did Jesus answer that one? Did he preach yet another sermon? No! 'In that hour he cured many of diseases and plagues and evil spirits, and on many that were blind he bestowed sight.' Here was a manifest demonstration of the good news that he had proclaimed. And this was his answer to John: 'Go and tell John what you have *seen and heard*: the blind receive their sight, the lame walk, lepers are cleansed, and the deaf hear, the dead are raised up, the poor have good news preached *(euaggelizontai)* to them.'[6]

Again in Luke, Chapter 8, we see the same warp and woof of evangelism. In the opening verse we find Jesus 'preaching *(kerusson)* and bringing the good news *(euaggelizomenos)* of the Kingdom of God'. What follows in the rest of the chapter? First there is powerful preaching in the parable of the sower; later the stilling of the storm on Lake Galilee; then the casting out of demons from Legion; then the healing of the woman with a haemorrhage; and then the raising of Jairus's daughter from the dead. What a way to bring the good news to the cities and villages of Galilee! This surely was a tremendously powerful part of Jesus's evangelism. It was neither the prelude to, nor the consequence of, evangelism. It was simply evangelism: the bringing of good news (as Paul described his own work in Romans 15:18f.) 'by word and deed, by the power of signs and wonders, by the power of the Holy Spirit'. Paul incidentally said that it was in this way that he had '*fully* preached the gospel of Christ'. The church today has had much experience in the 'word', a growing experience of 'deed', but all too little evidence of the power of signs and wonders or of the Holy Spirit.

Indeed the gospel records make it abundantly clear that you cannot separate, in the evangelistic ministry of Jesus, proclamation and demonstration, preaching and acting, saying and doing. In the first chapter of Mark's gospel we have the record of a typical day in the life of Jesus. The chapter starts. 'The beginning of the gospel *(euaggelion)* of Jesus Christ'. In 1:14f. we see Jesus 'preaching the gospel of God, and saying, "The time is fulfilled, and the Kingdom of God is at hand; repent, and believe in the gospel."' Then follows a series of incidents when he demonstrates the reality and power of the gospel: a man is delivered of an unclean spirit; Simon's mother-in-law is healed; many others are healed of their sicknesses and demons are cast out; a leper is cleansed; a paralytic leaps to his feet (at a time when Jesus was 'preaching the word'). This was of particular significance, as the healing indicated Christ's claim to have authority to forgive sins. Anyone could *say*, 'Your sins are forgiven', but not anyone could cause a paralysed man to rise to his feet and to walk out in front of the astonished crowd. Then, in almost the next recorded incident we find Jesus not only *saying* that he had come for sinners but scandalising his critics by actually eating a meal 'with tax collectors and sinners'. Constantly we find the living demonstration that he really meant what he said. He was demonstrating good news. As we have seen, we cannot take the verb 'to evangelise' out of its active and varied context without destroying a vital part of its meaning. It was never the bare proclamation of words. Always it was words set in action: not just 'signs and wonders', of course, but numerous examples of the love and care and compassion of the one who had come to bring good news. It is therefore not surprising that Luke says of his first volume: 'I have dealt with all that Jesus *began to do and teach.'*[7] Here the doing comes even before the teaching! And the implication of Luke's words is that Jesus went on doing and teaching through his Body, the Church.

This, in fact, is exactly what we find. Throughout the whole of Acts, in almost every chapter (the exceptions being mostly when Paul is making his defence), we see a demonstration accompanying the proclamation of the gospel. To give one example: in Acts, Chapter 8, the disciples, scattered after the persecution in Jerusalem, 'went about preaching *(euaggelizomenoi)* the word'. Philip, the evangelist, went to Samaria and proclaimed the Christ. 'And the multitudes with one accord gave heed to what was said by Philip, when they *heard* him and *saw* the signs which he did. For unclean spirits came out of many who were possessed, crying with a loud voice, and many who were paralysed or lame were healed.' Later Luke states that the Samaritans 'believed Philip as he preached good news *(euaggelizomeno)* about the Kingdom of God and the name of Jesus Christ'.[8] Here was powerful evangelism, not only because of the faithful announcement of the good news of God's Kingdom, but also because of the good deeds that accompanied the good words.

Most significant of all the passages, perhaps, is Acts 10:36-8. Here Peter is explaining the gospel in a setting he had never imagined possible: to Gentiles in the house of a Gentile, Cornelius. This remarkable crossing of the Jew-Gentile barrier in itself gave authenticity to the message that was to follow. And in a most striking way Peter talks about God, 'preaching good news *(euaggelizomenos)* of peace by Jesus Christ'. He then goes on to explain the word that was proclaimed (by God through Jesus): 'How God anointed Jesus of Nazareth with the Holy Spirit and with power; how he went about doing good and healing all that were oppressed by the devil.' Peter then spoke briefly about the death and resurrection of Jesus. This was God's action, evangelising through his Son Jesus Christ. It was not only the proclamation of his word that had become flesh, but also a word that was active and powerful in the lives of needy people. This, quite clearly, is a vital part of God's evangelistic work in the world through his Son: 'doing good and healing'.

Without some concrete reality of the gospel, words become empty and meaningless.

It is not surprising, therefore, that the same complaint against the Church is being voiced on all sides: 'The Church is suffocated with words and starved of experience'; 'The world is satiated with dogmas, but people are hungry for life'; 'Words, words, words — I'm sick of words... Show me.' In preparation for a town mission I was reminded recently by the committee that most people now had become 'word-resistant'. We shall return to this theme more fully in our next chapter, but from New Testament days to the twentieth century it remains true that, unless there is a demonstration of the power of the Spirit, the proclamation of the gospel will be in vain. It will not be evangelism.

Perhaps the most remarkable evangelistic mission I have had the privilege of leading illustrates this truth in vivid terms. I had been asked to 'proclaim the good news of Jesus Christ' both formally and informally, through services, house-meetings, youth fellowships and so forth. However, the context of this proclamation of words had been very rich indeed. In the two churches involved there had been a gracious and powerful move of the Spirit of God. This had led to much prayer, an increasing experience of some of the hitherto unknown gifts of the Spirit (such as prophecy, healing, tongues with interpretation), small fellowship groups meeting regularly, a healthy involvement in the community, and, above all, a warm, loving, welcoming, caring fellowship of God's people — an effective body of Christ. During the long weekend of that mission the spiritual harvest was quite remarkable: approximately a hundred men and women professed faith in Christ on one day alone, and I understand that not only was there 100 per cent turn-out for the follow-up meeting a few days afterwards, but God's work in those churches has gone on from strength to strength. Although it is certainly true that we must not measure evangelism in terms of apparent 'success', it is equally true that here was a full and powerful proclamation of the good news of Jesus Christ 'by word and deed, by the power of signs and wonders, by the power of the Holy Spirit'. No wonder Christ was able to 'win obedience' amongst so many!

In other evangelistic services or missions, I have seen the immense power of worship and praise preceding the more formal presentation of the gospel. We shall return to this later, but often, after twenty or thirty minutes of songs that are specifically God-directed worship in their content, there is a sense of God's presence which wonderfully enables people to hear and receive the spoken word of God. After all, Pentecost began not with preaching but with praise. 'A praising community preaches to answer questions raised by its praise.'[9]

That is a neat and profound statement. All too often people are not asking questions about God at all. They are simply apathetic. But when you begin to see ordinary men and women absorbed in something, excited about something, joyful about something, in love with something, singing about something, you will naturally want to know what that something is. Questions will then be asked, which is a vital prelude to receiving the good news of Christ.

It is also worth noticing briefly that the verb 'to evangelise' is used occasionally for those *inside* the Kingdom, as well as for those outside. In Romans 1:15, for example, Paul wrote: 'So I am eager to preach the gospel *(euaggelisasthai)* to you also who are in Rome'; and by 'you' he meant 'God's beloved in Rome, who are called to be saints' (verse 7). For the time being he had to content himself with sending them a letter. And what a letter! Here is a magnificent exposition of the gospel, and subsequent generations have proved how intensely relevant this is for believers as well as for unbelievers. The gospel affects every part of our life. Michael Green once described the gospel as being like the sea: a child can paddle in the shallows, but even a giraffe is soon out of its depths. The more we grow spiritually, the more profound the gospel becomes. It never ceases to be relevant, comforting and challenging. Although it may be a rare use of the word, it is biblical to talk about evangelising Christians! Even the most mature in the faith need to have the gospel, with all its simplicity yet profundity, preached to them. Until we enjoy fully 'the glorious liberty of the children of God', and until we see clearly 'his glorious inheritance in the saints', with all that immeasurable power which is available to us who believe, we do not outgrow the need for the good news to be preached to us: release to the captives, sight to the blind, and liberty to the oppressed.

The Gospel

The noun *(euaggelion)*[10] occurs seventy-two times in the New Testament, fifty-four of which come in Paul's writings. From these passages we can learn the following truths about the gospel that is to be proclaimed in evangelism.

(i)   It is the gospel of the *Kingdom*.[11] This expression has often caused debate and confusion. Some equate God's Kingdom with society and social order, so that God's Kingdom comes through the exercise of social justice. Others see God's Kingdom wholly in the future, referring to the new heavens and new earth in which only righteousness dwells. Others equate it with the Church militant, in heaven and on earth. No doubt all these ideas are involved in the concept of the Kingdom, but the primary biblical idea of the Kingdom is the authority and rule of the King. Of course Christ will one day have complete authority over all, and is today concerned about social justice; but basically the word refers simply to the sovereignty of the King, who has the authority to rule: 'The Lord has established his throne in the heavens, and his Kingdom (i.e. his authority or power) rules over all.'[12] And it is particularly significant that the first two references to the gospel of the Kingdom are in the context of Christ's manifest authority over the powers of evil. In both Matthew 4:23 and 9:35 we see Jesus 'preaching the gospel of the Kingdom and healing every disease and every infirmity among the people'. Moreover, although the fact of Christ's rule involves the challenging command to obey him, it is really good news to know that someone is in control of this world and of our own personal lives. It is good news to know that, in every situation, however chaotic, disastrous, distressing or painful it may seem to be, Jesus is Lord. 'The Lord reigns; let the earth rejoice,' sings the psalmist. Nothing is finally outside his sovereign control. He has the whole world in his hands.

(ii) It is the gospel of *God*.[13] This is so in two senses. In the first place the good news is *about* God: it speaks of an infinite, personal God who so loved the world that he gave his only Son for us, who longs to reconcile us to himself, who yearns to be a Father to us, and who sends the Spirit of his Son into our hearts, crying 'Abba! Father!' For those who are searching for God and who are lost in the labyrinth of religious ideas, the gospel certainly contains good news about God. In the second place it is good news *from* God. It is both his initiative and his revelation. Man, left to himself, could neither find God nor know the truth about God. But God has graciously revealed himself. It is therefore essentially God's gospel, not man's.[14] God has spelt out *his* truth. It is above all *his* good news. In view of this, any twist, distortion or alteration to the gospel made by man is extremely serious: 'If any one is preaching to you a gospel contrary to that which you received, let him be accursed.'[15] Indeed, if 'ignorant and unstable' men twist the Scriptures in any way, they do so 'to their own destruction'.[16]

(iii) It is the gospel of *Jesus Christ*.[17] Again it is good news in two senses. First, Jesus *brought* it into the world. Without him there would be no good news at all. Apart from the specific revelation given to the Jews through the law and prophets, the world would have continued to sit in spiritual darkness. The 'times of ignorance' would go on indefinitely. Secondly, Jesus *embodied* the gospel. Here was a stupendous piece of drama: the word of God dramatically displayed on earth. Indeed, because he was the Word made flesh he could make that astonishing claim: 'He who has seen me has seen the Father.'[18] Now at last we can know the truth about God because we can see the truth in Jesus.

(iv) It is a gospel that must be *personally appropriated*. Paul sometimes talks of 'our' gospel, or even 'my' gospel.[19] Until there has been a wholehearted personal response to the gospel, so that we not only believe it but also hold it fast, the gospel itself is in vain.[20]

Moreover this response must be a total one, equivalent to losing one's life, being unashamed of the gospel, doing all 'for the sake of the gospel', and even being willing to leave house and family 'for the gospel'.[21] Further, since there must be a free and willing response, tragically it is possible to miss it, neglect it, disobey it or refuse it.[22] Love always risks being rejected, and it is one essential part of God's love that he solemnly respects man's freedom of choice. Indeed the nature of his judgment is that he underlines the decision that we make about him. The fact of the gospel gives us no ground whatsoever to 'presume upon the riches of his Kingdom and forbearance and patience. Do you not know,' asks Paul, 'that God's kindness is meant to lead you to repentance?'[23]

(v)   It is a gospel *for all men*.[24] God knows nothing of the barriers of class, creed or culture; he wills that all should reach repentance and be saved. 'He bestows his riches upon all who call upon him. For, "every one who calls upon the name of the Lord will be saved."'[25] Therefore the gospel must be shared with others.[26] A student once asked Charles Spurgeon if the heathen who had never heard the gospel would be saved. Spurgeon answered, 'It is more a question with me whether we who hear the gospel, and fail to give it to those who have not, can be saved.'[27] Indeed, the task of evangelism must at all costs *not* be neglected, since the gospel has been 'entrusted' to us and 'laid upon' us, so that we are now called to 'serve' the gospel.[28] As William Barclay very neatly expresses it: 'A man must give his life to that which gave him life.' Further, the responsibility to spread the gospel is such a solemn and urgent one that Paul took the greatest pains, regardless of personal cost or suffering, to make quite sure that he would never 'put an obstacle' in the way of it.[29]

The noun 'evangelist' (euaggelistes). This occurs only three times in the New Testament, referring to Philip, to Timothy and to some who would be given this ministry within the Body of

Christ, for the benefit of the whole Body.[30] From this, although evangelism is a prime responsibility of the whole Church, and to that extent all Christians are to be involved in evangelism, not all Christians are called to be evangelists. All Christians belong to the Church, which is inescapably involved in evangelism, but many Christians will find their primary sphere of service *within* the Body of Christ. Here they are to love and serve one another as God directs and as the Spirit distributes gifts, in order that the Body as a whole may be strengthened and better equipped to proclaim Christ to the world. But within the Church some will be especially called to be evangelists, just as some may have a prophetic ministry, and others will be pastors and teachers. It is the gift of God that makes a man an evangelist. Others may equally be able to explain the gospel, but the evangelist will have both the burden to evangelise and that God-given ability to communicate the gospel effectively to others. This gift, like all other gifts and ministries, should become obvious to, and recognised by, the Church. As this is one of the gifts 'for building up the Body of Christ', no man should be a self-styled evangelist, but one who is acknowledged and encouraged in this ministry by the body of Christians whom he serves.

2. PROCLAMATION

'To proclaim' *(kerussein),* 'proclamation' *(kerugma),* and 'herald' *(kerux).* The verb, meaning 'to preach' or 'to proclaim', is used as commonly as the verb 'to evangelise', coming sixty-one times in the New Testament. The proclamation *(kerugma)* comes eight times, and the preacher *(kerux)* only three. The basic idea behind these words is that of a herald who delivers a message that has been given to him by the king. Senft expresses this well in von Allmen's *Vocabulary of the Bible:*

> *To preach,* especially, has lost for us its primitive meaning, since it suggests a discourse more or less personal, more or less doctrinal and theoretical, addressed to a closed group of convinced believers within the precincts of the church,

and that is the very opposite of what it ought to suggest and indeed of what the original word means: a proclamation made by a herald, by the town crier, in the full light of day, to the sound of a trumpet, up-to-the-minute, addressed to everyone because it comes from the king himself... Of a herald the chief requirement is absolute fidelity; he does not have to express his own ideas, but to deliver a message laid upon him; he is not asked for his opinion on the questions at issue, he is merely the mouthpiece of him who has commissioned him. By this very fact he is invested with the authority which he represents and his speech is endowed with an unquestionable prestige. The herald is nothing in himself; he speaks as representative of the one who has sent him and on behalf of the message which has been entrusted to him.[31]

The word *kerugma,* or the message that is proclaimed, is equated by Paul with *euaggelion,* the gospel. This becomes especially clear in Romans 16:25: 'Now to him who is able to strengthen you according to my gospel *(euaggelion)* and the preaching *(kerugma)* of Jesus Christ.' From the context it is plain that he saw his gospel and Christ's preaching as one and the same message: it is the fulfilment of the prophetic writings, given by God, with universal application, calling for the obedience of faith. However, when writing to the Corinthians, Paul emphasised that his *kerugma* was utterly different from the studied rhetoric and flowery eloquence of the professional Greek sophist. No doubt these travelling lecturers, with their impressive flow of lofty words, gave all the appearance of wisdom, but in God's eyes it was all empty foolishness. Paul, however, saw that his task was to herald God's message of 'Christ crucified', even though it would be a stumbling block to Jews and folly to Greeks. He knew Christ to be the power and wisdom of God, and therefore, pushing firmly to one side the showy techniques of the Greek philosophers, 'my speech and my message *(kerugma)* were not in plausible words of wisdom, but in demonstration of the Spirit and power, that your faith might not rest in the wisdom of men but in the power of God'.[32] Unlike the 'debater of this age', whose skill was to play with words, Paul delivered a message rooted in the historical facts of Jesus Christ, notably his death and resurrection. This is why his words had such power: he was proclaiming the living Christ, who had risen from the dead. Indeed, as he went on to explain later in his letter, 'if Christ has not been raised, then our preaching *(kerugma)* is in vain and your faith is in vain.'[33]

Theologians for years have debated whether or not there was a fixed *kerugma* which was always to be found in the evangelistic preaching of the early Church. Some detect three essential points in the apostolic gospel, and others five, six or seven. Michael Green summarises the debate in ten helpful pages in his excellent book *Evangelism in the Early Church*.[34] Probably the most accurate conclusion is that

> all Christians were convinced that Jesus Christ was God's last word to man, the one who brought as much of God to us as we could appreciate in the only terms we could take it in, the terms of a human life; the one who in dying and rising again was manifestly vindicated in his claims and achievements. This they all believed in common: their modes of expressing it depended to a large extent on their own intellectual and spiritual background and on that of their hearers.[35]

Perhaps the difficulty in summarising the apostolic message stems from the fact that, in proclaiming the word, the apostles were not so much declaring Bible words or a gospel formula, as proclaiming Jesus Christ himself: 'We preach *(kerussomen)* Jesus Christ as Lord.'[36] John Wesley wrote in his *Journal* for July 17th, 1739: 'I rode to Bradford 5 miles from Bath. Some persons had pitched on a convenient place, on the top of the hill under which the town lies; there I offered Christ to about 1,000 people, for wisdom, righteousness, sanctification and redemption.' Certainly our words and doctrines need to be right; but to 'preach the word' is basically to offer people Christ.

Professor James Stewart captures the vitality of true preaching in his book on this subject:

Ernest Raymond, novelist and essayist, has described the most impressive sermon he ever heard. In itself, he relates, the sermon was ordinary enough: intellectually negligible, aesthetically ragged. Its construction was faulty, its delivery abominable. Yet its effect was overwhelming... 'I think he spoke for an hour, and not a man of us moved, and most of us were very quiet all that night...' It is one thing to learn the technique and mechanics of preaching: it is quite another to preach a sermon which will draw back the veil and make the barriers fall that hide the face of God.[37]

That is ultimately the task of the evangelist and herald, and to this end he must be not only faithful to the message entrusted to him, but also dependent on the Holy Spirit who alone can glorify Christ and bring the hearers in touch with the living God.

NOTES

1 Archbishops' Committee of Enquiry on the Evangelistic Work of the Church, p.25.
2 *Evangelism and the Sovereignty of God* (I.V.P.), 40, p. 25.
3 The Lausanne Covenant, from *Let the Earth hear His Voice* (World Wide Publications), 4, p. 25.
4 *On the Other Side* (Scripture Union), 61, p. 26.
5 Psalm 40:10; 96:2, p. 26.
6 Luke 7:19-22, p. 27.
7 Acts 1:1, p. 29.
8 Acts 8:6-7, 12, p. 29.
9 Comment made by Roland Walls during a conference for university chaplains in Durham in 1973, p. 31.
10 For an excellent study of this word, see W. Barclay, *A New Testament Wordbook* (S.C.M.), 41-6. The author acknowledges help from this, p. 32.
11 Matthew 4:23; 9:35; 24:14, p. 32.
12 Psalm 103:19, p. 32.
13 Mark 1:14; I Thessalonians 2:2, 8, 9, p. 33.
14 See Galatians 1:11-12; 1 Corinthians 2:9-11, p. 33.
15 See Galatians 1:6-9; 2 Corinthians 11:4, p. 33.
16 2 Peter 3:16, p. 33.
17 Mark 1:1; 2 Corinthians 4:4; 9:13; 10:14, p. 33.
18 John 14:9, p. 33.
19 2 Corinthians 4:3; 1 Thessalonians 1:5; 2 Thessalonians 2:14, p. 33.

20   1 Corinthians 15:1-2; cf. Mark 1:14-15, p. 33.
21   Mark 8:35; Romans 1:16; 1 Corinthians 9:23;
     Mark 10:29, p.34
22   Romans 2:16; 10:16; 2 Thessalonians 1:7-8; 1 Peter
     4;17, p. 34.
23   Romans 2:4-5, p. 34.
24   Mark 13:10; 16:15; Acts 15:7, p. 34.
25   Romans 10:12-13, p. 34.
26   Romans 15:19; 1 Corinthians 9:14, 18;
     2 Corinthians 10:14; 11:7; Galatians 2:2, p. 34.
27   Told in O.J. Sanders, *What of the Unevangelized?*
     (O.M.F.), 80, p. 34.
28   1 Thessalonians 2:4; I Corinthians 9:16;
     Romans 1:1; 15:16; *et al*, p. 34.
29   1 Corinthians 9:12, p. 34.
30   Acts 21:8; 2 Timothy 4:5; Ephesians 4:11, p. 35.
31   Op.cit., 335, p. 35.
32   1 Corinthians 1:18-2:5, p. 36.
33   1 Corinthians 15:14, p. 37.
34   Hodder & Stoughton, 60-70, p. 37.
35   Op. cit., 63, p. 37.
36   2 Corinthians 4:5, p. 37.
37   *Teach Yourself Preaching*, 88f, p. 37.

CHAPTER THREE

The Word in Evangelism

THE WORD OF GOD

'THE WORD' is a phrase that has become familiar jargon in certain Christian circles. 'That was a good word tonight!' says a church member to the preacher when the service is over. 'Does he preach the word?' asks a Christian concerning the biblical soundness' of a minister.

However good or bad the jargon may be, it is certainly biblical. In describing the evangelistic work of the Church in the Acts of the Apostles, Luke used 'the word' more than fifty times.[1] The disciples prayed that they might 'speak thy word with all boldness', and when they were filled with the Holy Spirit that is precisely what happened.[2] After the persecution in Jerusalem, those who were scattered 'went about preaching the word';[3] Paul and Barnabas, on their first missionary journey 'proclaimed the word of God'[4] in the synagogues at Salamis in Cyprus; and later Paul spent eighteen months 'teaching the word of God' at Corinth.[5] So important was this task that the apostles knew they must not 'neglect the preaching of God's word in order to handle finances', however pressing some of the pastoral and practical needs might be; it was their task to devote themselves to prayer and to the 'ministry of the word'.[6]

Likewise, at the receiving end, the whole city of Antioch came together to 'hear the word of God';[7] both the Samaritans and the Gentiles 'received the word of God';[8] and again at Antioch they were so thrilled with the good news of God's salvation that they 'glorified the word of God'.[9] In Acts, Luke speaks variously of 'the word of God', 'the word of the Lord', 'the word of his grace', or just 'the word'.

Further, it is of particular interest that Luke, in describing the evangelistic success of the Church, says 'the word of God increased',[10] 'the word of God grew and multiplied',[11] 'the word of the Lord spread',[12] and 'the word of the Lord grew and prevailed mightily'.[13] This is such a remarkable way of recording the growth of the Church that Calvin in his Commentary says of Acts 19:20, 'The word *grew* do I refer unto the number of men, as if he should have said that the Church was increased.' However, Luke on all four occasions says 'the word' and not 'the church', possibly for this reason: just as Jesus was the Word made flesh, so the Church as the Body of Christ is, in one sense, the Word made flesh. As we shall see later, one vital means of communication between God and the world is the Church: thus when the Church increased, it is of particular significance to say that 'the word increased'.

1.   WHAT IS 'THE WORD'?

Throughout the Scriptures the word of God is always seen as something which lives and acts:

> For as the rain and the snow come down from heaven, and return not thither but water the earth, making it bring forth and sprout, giving seed to the sower and bread to the eater, so shall my word be that goes forth from my mouth; it shall not return to me empty, but it shall accomplish that which I purpose, and prosper in the thing for which I have sent it.[14]

The New Testament bears the same witness. Paul said about the gospel, as he preached it to the Thessalonians, that it 'came to you not only in word, but also in power and in the Holy Spirit and with full conviction'; indeed, they received his message as 'the word of God, which is at work in you believers'.[15] Peter, too, reminded his readers that they had been 'born anew...through the living and abiding word of God'. And after quoting from Isaiah 40 to assure them that, unlike human frailty, the word of the Lord really does abide for ever, he wrote, 'That word is the good news which was preached to you.'[16] The writer to Hebrews also stresses that 'the word of God is living and active, sharper than any two-edged sword, piercing to the division of soul and spirit, of joints and marrow, and discerning the thoughts and intentions of the heart.'[17] This is particularly interesting, since it shows that we cannot separate the word of God from the living God. The word is living and active because God is living and active; the word discerns the thoughts and intentions of the heart because God does just that. Indeed, after this statement about 'the word', the next verse begins, 'And before *him* no creature is hidden.'

Since the nineteenth-century days of C. Hodge and B. B. Warfield there has, in some circles, been a very precise correspondence between 'the word of God' and the Scriptures: a one-to-one identification, in fact. Undoubtedly the Scriptures play a most vital part in God's revelation of himself to man. They form the supreme objective authority for what God has said. We see this very clearly in the teachings of Jesus. Basically there are three claims of authority for what we believe and how we behave: Scripture, reason, and tradition. However, Jesus not only knew the Scriptures, revered the Scriptures, fulfilled the Scriptures, lived by the Scriptures and taught the Scriptures; he also rebuked the rationalists of his day for letting reason dominate their beliefs: 'You are wrong, because you know neither the Scriptures nor the power of God';[18] and he corrected the traditionalists, when their traditions clashed with the word of God: 'You leave the commandment of God, and hold fast the tradition of men...thus making void the word of God through your tradition.'[19] Both reason and tradition, therefore, must bow to the supreme authority of Scripture, which is the word of God. There is no doubt about the immense importance of Scripture when it comes to God's communication to man.[20]

Nevertheless, in the Bible the 'word of God' is seen as greater than 'Bible words', however important those words are as an objective statement of divine truth. For example, it is by the word of God that the heavens and earth were created;[21] in Jesus Christ 'the Word became flesh and dwelt

among us, full of grace and truth';[22] and it is through Jesus
that God has spoken to us.[23] Moreover, God has spoken 'in
many and various ways', not just through the Scriptures. For
example, David in Psalm 19 talks of God's revelation both in
his creation and in his word. Vividly he describes creation as
the silent eloquence of God's word:

> The heavens are *telling* the glory of God;
> And the firmament *proclaims* his handiwork,
> Day to day pours forth *speech,*
> And night to night *declares* knowledge;
> There is no speech, nor are there words;
> Their voice is not heard;
> Yet their *voice* goes out through all the earth,
> And their *words* to the end of the world.

God's silent word, coming to us visually instead of audibly,
is something we need increasingly to remember in an age
dominated by television, glossy magazines and the popular
daily newspapers. The creative arts have a vital part to play
in proclaiming the Word which once became flesh. Drama,
dance, mime, painting, photography, architecture, tapestry:
all of these can tell the glory of God and proclaim his
handiwork. At times a silent presentation of God's truth can
speak much more loudly than words. Paul also makes it clear
that God has already revealed himself, even to those without
the special revelation of his written word, both in creation
and in conscience.[24] Here God has 'shown' them the truth; he
has 'written' his law on their hearts.

From this it is clear that the 'word of God' is not to be
taken as precisely identical with Scriptures alone; it is God's
communication of himself to man. It includes 'the many and
various ways' in which he reveals 'his eternal power and
deity', his 'grace and truth', his salvation and his judgment.
Indeed, because God is the living God who thinks and feels
and speaks and acts, his communication with living people,
who being made in God's image also think and feel and speak
and act, is inevitably complex and varied. The vital point is
that it is God revealing himself to man, God giving us 'a spirit
of wisdom and of revelation in the knowledge of him',[25] God

speaking or acting in such a way that we can say that it 'communicates'. The word of God without God is nonsense. 'The written code kills'; it is only 'the Spirit who gives life'.[26] Therefore, before biblical words can become the living and active word of God, the operation of the Holy Spirit is essential.

It is interesting to see how clearly this was understood by the Reformers, who rediscovered the central importance of the written word of God. François Wendel, Dean of Theology at the University of Strasbourg and a noted expert on the Reformation, made this pertinent comment on Calvin's understanding of Scripture:

> Of itself Scripture is nothing but the dead letter, like any other historical document. Before we can find the living word of God in it, and have assurance that this word is personally addressed to each one of us, there must be an intervention of the Holy Spirit. It is the Holy Spirit who makes use of the Biblical writings to put us in contact with the word of God, and who at the same time works within us so that we may discover this word in the Scripture and accept it as coming from God. In a celebrated passage, Calvin has defined what is meant by this operation of the Holy Spirit, its bearing witness in the soul of every believer to the truth and authenticity of the Scripture: 'Though indeed God alone is sufficient witness to himself in his word, nevertheless that word will obtain no credence in the heart of man if it be not sealed by the interior witness of the Spirit... Wherefore it is necessary that the same Spirit who spoke by the mouth of the Prophet must enter into our own hearts and touch them to the quick, in order to persuade them that the Prophets have faithfully set forth that which was commanded them from on high.[27]

It is because of this truth that Paul knew the paramount importance, when preaching the gospel of 'Christ crucified', that there should be a 'demonstration of the Spirit and power'; only then could the faith of those who believed rest not in the wisdom of men but in the power of God.[28] Indeed, unless this power of the Spirit was present, he would not truly be proclaiming the word of God, however true he might be to Scripture. Although evangelistic preaching in Acts naturally included Old Testament quotations (particularly when proclaiming the word of God to Jews), there was, together with the focal points of the gospel,[29] a relevance and application that made for real communication with those who heard. Therefore 'preaching the word' is never just faithfulness to biblical words (many a sound sermon has sent people sound asleep!), but through the activity of the Spirit it is God's word to those people on that occasion. Naturally, by the Spirit, that same sermon can be God's word to different people on a different occasion; but the essential point is that it is God revealing himself to man.

2. THE WORD OF GOD FOR THE EARLY CHURCH

In the Acts of the Apostles we see the tremendously rich means of communication between God and man, making the traditional picture of the preacher proclaiming the word from the pulpit astonishingly restrictive. How was the word of God made known in first-century evangelism?

PREACHING AND TEACHING

In recognising that 'the word' is not to be restricted to Scripture, we must not in any way minimise the verbal proclamation of biblical truth. It was not enough for the Holy Spirit to fall on the disciples at Pentecost: the crowd had to understand what it was all about. Peter therefore explained briefly the prophecy of Joel, and preached Jesus Christ, calling on the crowd to repent, believe, and receive the Holy Spirit. It was not enough for the cripple to be healed (in Acts 3): again Peter preached Christ, and urged men to repent and believe. We shall see in Chapter 4 something of the content of the message proclaimed, but at this stage it is worth noting three facts. In the first place Luke uses a wide variety of words to describe evangelistic preaching. Two of these have already been examined in our previous chapter: the apostles 'preached the gospel' *(euaggelizesthai)* and 'heralded the Christ' *(kerussein)*. They also 'testified the word of the Lord' *(diamarturasthai)*, and 'proclaimed the word of God' *(kataggel-lein)*, and in all these verbs there is the thought of an announcement: bringing a message, bearing the authority of the King, to those who need to hear and know the truth. Sometimes in evangelistic missions I say, in passing, 'I am not asking whether or not you believe this or agree with this; I am simply telling you what Jesus said and did.' Today, as in New Testament times, there is widespread ignorance about the basic facts and evidences of the Christian faith. Before any profitable discussion or debate can take place we need to declare the good news of Jesus Christ.

In connection with this Luke makes frequent use of the verb 'to teach' *(didaskein)*,[30] indicating that apostles spent time, whenever possible, instructing their hearers in 'the whole counsel of God'. They sought to omit nothing 'that was profitable'. Indeed, in Acts, Chapter 20, Paul twice says about this that he 'did not shrink' from this *(hupostellein)*. This is a word sometimes used in nautical circles for pulling down a sail. Out of fear of man it is all too easy to pull down the sails and shrink from certain aspects of the whole counsel of God that might be unpopular or unfashionable in either secular or religious circles. But with the wind of the Spirit blowing strongly, the apostles refused to pull down their sails in their faithful teaching of the word of God. Indeed, so powerful was it that Jewish leaders protested, 'You have filled Jerusalem with your teaching.'[31] Certainly they often 'exhorted' their hearers to respond,[32] but they knew the importance of instructing the mind with the truth, as well as moving the heart and bending the will. This is further seen by the way the apostles, in that appeal to an intellectual understanding of the gospel, used 'to argue' *(dialegesthai)*,[33] often arguing from the Scriptures with the Jews, seeking to prove that Jesus was the Christ, but sometimes arguing with Gentiles, for example about 'justice and self-control and future judgment'. They also used 'to dispute' *(suzetein)*,[34] 'to confound' *(sugchun-ein)*,[35] 'to prove' *(sumbibazein* and *paratithemi)*,[36] and 'to confute powerfully' *(diakatelegchein)*,[37] In all this the apostles were profoundly aware of the importance or urgency of their message. God's word could be either received or rejected, and because of this they brought both salvation and judgment to those who heard.[38] It was therefore their solemn and earnest intention, maintaining their integrity as those who were in no wise 'peddlers of God's word', to 'persuade' *(peithein)* men of the truth of what they proclaimed.[39]

In the second place, it is worth noting the apostles' thoroughness and persistence in their evangelistic work. Although they moved from city to city on their missionary journeys, they spent as much time as possible proclaiming, teaching, arguing and persuading. For example, in Acts 14:3 Paul and Barnabas, when in Iconium, 'remained for a long time, speaking boldly for the Lord', for the Lord was manifestly with them as he 'bore witness to the word of his grace, granting signs and wonders to be done by their hands'. In Thessalonica Paul 'for three weeks argued with them from the Scriptures'.[40] At Corinth 'we argued in the synagogue every sabbath... And he stayed a year and six months, teaching the word of God among them.'[41] Perhaps most impressive of all was at Ephesus where 'he entered the synagogue and for three months spoke boldly, arguing and pleading about the kingdom of God', and, on top of that, for two years he 'argued daily in the hall of Tyrannus'.[42] Some manuscripts add that he did this 'from the fifth hour to the tenth', and, if this is correct, I wonder how many other evangelists since then have spent five hours a day for two years in one place 'pleading about the kingdom of God'! It is hardly surprising that it was at Ephesus that 'God did extraordinary miracles by the hands of Paul', that there was a great bonfire of expensive books on the occult, and that 'the word of the Lord grew and prevailed mightily.' Further, when Paul was in open house-arrest in Rome, 'great numbers' of Jewish leaders came to him, and 'he expounded the matter to them from morning to evening, testifying to the kingdom of God and trying to convince them about Jesus both from the law of Moses and from the prophets'. After that 'he lived there two whole years at his own expense, and welcomed all who came to him, preaching the kingdom of God and teaching about the Lord Jesus quite openly and unhindered.'[43]

In the third place, it is fascinating to see that opportunities for evangelism were snatched up in almost every conceivable place. Most often the apostles proclaimed the word of God in the temple[44] and synagogue.[45] There especially, of course, they would find those who at least professed to believe in God and who knew something of the Scriptures. And it needs to be remembered today that the Church is all too often a pool to fish in, rather than a boat to fish from. However, frequent use was also made of the home,[46] and this still is undoubtedly one of the best of all settings for evangelism. Frequently I have seen the value of the home, with gatherings ranging from 6 to 150, and usually from 20 to 40. Here is the ideal framework for genuine communication, providing an opportunity for declaring the good news of Christ, together with come-back, discussion, debate, argument and spontaneous testimony from other Christians present. It is a relaxed environment for those who might feel uncomfortable and on the defensive in a church building. It is the time and place when many personal doubts and difficulties can be expressed and, perhaps, resolved. At such a gathering a few weeks before this page was written, a fine man found a living faith in Christ, partly by being able to talk personally with several Christian friends who were present; another agnostic, who argued fairly heatedly at the time, now describes himself as 'on the brink' of commitment. The home is a marvellous field for evangelism, and Christians who catch the vision of this have an immense contribution to make for the Kingdom of God today.

Nevertheless, it is challenging to see that those first disciples took every conceivable opportunity they could to proclaim Christ, whatever the personal risk involved: before the powerful body of the Jewish Sanhedrin,[47] on the steps of the famous Areopagus,[48] in the Roman court of proconsul Sergius Paulus,[49] during the tribunals of Felix, governor of Judea,[50] and of Festus even when King Agrippa and Bernice were present,[51] in the chariot of the Ethiopian Chancellor of the Exchequer,[52] and also in prison,[53] in the public lecture hall of Tyrannus[54] and in the market place of Athens.[55] It is worth noticing that the apostles usually spoke in response to invitations, although sometimes they took obvious steps to elicit such invitations. They also spoke in 'cities and villages', and they seemed to welcome opportunities with the large crowds as well as with the small home-meeting: 'almost the whole city gathered together to hear the word of God'.[56] It is impossible to detect any of the careful methods and strategies that so characterise evangelistic campaigns of today. Rather, as the Spirit moved and as God gave the opening, so the apostles grasped every opportunity they could for preaching and teaching the gospel of Christ. This was the first and foremost means of making known God's word to God's world. However, it was not the only means.

A LOVING, UNITED CHURCH

The supreme revelation of God is, of course, to be found in Jesus when 'the Word became flesh.' However, although Jesus had a deep and profound experience of the living God by his perfect oneness with him, he was no detached mystic. Indeed, it was the ordinary folk, the working man and the oppressed who especially found him so attractive. It was these people who had little time for the established, formal religion of the day (how little have things changed in 2,000 years!), because, frankly, the establishment had little real concern for them. But when Jesus came to preach good news to the poor, and to set at liberty those who were oppressed, that really got through. His whole life-style, the simplicity of his teaching, his obvious compassion, his reality and integrity — all this communicated to the man in the street in a most convincing way. The Word in becoming flesh was so powerful that if you did not accept it you could only seek to destroy it.

Further, there is a sense in which the Word must always become flesh before the living God can be clearly seen by a world that initially could not care less about biblical words. '*Show* us the Father, and we shall be satisfied,' is still the cry of the agnostic today. 'We wish to *see* Jesus.' The question is, how can people 'see God'? There are two illuminating verses in the New Testament, both of which begin with the words 'No one has ever seen God'. Of course that is true, for God dwells in unapproachable light; no sinful man could see God and live. The first verse is John 1:18: 'No one has ever seen God; the only Son, who is in the bosom of the Father, he has made him known.' 2,000 years ago God revealed himself in the person of his Son. The other reference is I John 4:12: 'No man has ever seen God; if we love one another, God abides in us.' Thus God reveals himself today through the body of Christ, the Church, when we love one another. Nothing today is more powerful than this. When our life-style and relationships with one another reflect the reality and beauty of Jesus, this will communicate to most people, especially those disillusioned by the establishment, more effectively than all the eloquent preaching in the world. Indeed the 'Body (soma) of Christ' for Paul was far more than a graphic analogy of internal relationships. 'For Paul soma is primarily the corporeality in which man lives in this world. It is thus the chance to meet others. For Paul then, the Body of Christ is in the first instance the Body given for others.'[57] In other words, it is through his Body, the Church, that Christ today expresses himself to the world. In part, at least, this is the evidence for the resurrection of Christ that the world needs to see.

This was certainly true in the New Testament Church. See the warmth and vitality of the Church, following the outpouring of the Spirit at Pentecost. Here they were worshipping, studying and praying together, selling their possessions, giving to those in need, and constantly in and out of each other's homes, sharing together their meals. No wonder that 'the Lord added to their number day by day those who were being saved.'[58]

A woman wrote to me once after an ordinary evening service in our church in York: 'One of the most wonderful things was to look around at the faces of the congregation — they were so relaxed, so absorbed, so open and content, and of course all this created the most incredible, almost tangible, atmosphere... It seemed to solidify so many things for me. If I had any doubts before your service, all that it showed us would have quite decided me about the reality of Christ.' She went on to speak warmly about the sermon (given by a well-known preacher), but it was the whole service and congregation that communicated Christ to this woman. Therefore at times local churches need to concentrate on strengthening relationships within the Body of Christ. This will not waste valuable time that could have been better used for evangelism; rather it will greatly increase the power of God's word that is proclaimed in and from that church.

In this increasingly cold and bleak world, what people are wanting and needing first and foremost is warmth — the warmth of love and acceptance and joy. They need to feel God's presence before they will listen to God's word. More than anything the Church needs to become a loving, caring, welcoming fellowship which radiates the joy of Jesus Christ. Someone who has worked extensively amongst Communists has said that those who have been won for Christ attribute their conversion always to the love of God manifested in the lives of God's people and seldom to being out-argued. So often today it is the pub, the working-man's club, the Bingo hall, that reflect the acceptance and joy that others need — not the Church. Bruce Larson once put it like this:

> The neighbourhood bar is possibly the best counterfeit there is to the fellowship Christ wants to give his Church. It's an invitation, dispensing liquor instead of grace, escape rather than reality, but it is a permissive, accepting and inclusive fellowship. It is unshockable. It is democratic. You can tell people secrets and they usually don't tell others or even want to. The bar flourishes not because most people are alcoholics, but because God has put into the human heart the desire to know and be known, to love and be loved, and so many seek a counterfeit at the price of a few beers. Christ wants his Church to be unshockable, democratic, permissive — a fellowship where people can come in and say 'I'm beat!' 'I've had it!' Alcoholics Anonymous has this quality. Our churches too often miss it.[59]

Again, a report from the Archbishops' Council for Evangelism made the point that modern language and new forms of service will never draw the multitude into church. What is crucial, however, is that if and when the outsider does come he discovers there a loving, caring community and 'one which is obviously in love with God and offering real worship'. Today there is a hunger for reality. And it is the reality of love and worship which is intangible but unmistakable, and has a vital part to play in evangelism. The importance too of loving Christian communities and extended families cannot be over-emphasised, particularly in a generation which sees a wholesale and tragic breakdown of relationships at almost every level. But more about this in a later chapter.

SIGNS AND WONDERS

Unquestionably this was an integral part of proclaiming the word of God in New Testament times. Confronted by the pagan mixture of materialism, rationalism and occultism, people needed a demonstration of the power of Christ. Although Paul was wary of this demand for signs,[60] knowing that often this was little more than an attempt to evade the personal challenge of Christ, he still knew the value of signs and wonders in his evangelistic work.[61] Almost every chapter in Acts records some manifestation of the Spirit: tongues, healings, prophecies, visions, judgments, exorcisms, miracles — all of which were powerful ways of helping people to come to a living faith in a living God. Why did the vast crowd gather round the disciples at Pentecost? Because 'we hear them telling in our own tongues the mighty works of God.' Why were 2,000 more converted shortly afterwards? Partly because 'many wonders and signs were done through the apostles', including the healing of a cripple from birth, who went 'walking and leaping and praising God' in the temple, so that all the people 'were filled with wonder and amazement'.[62]

J. B. Phillips, in his preface to his paraphrase of the Acts of the Apostles, put it like this:

> These men did not make 'acts of faith', they believed; they did not 'say their prayers', they really prayed. They did not hold conferences on psychosomatic medicine, they simply healed the sick... No one can read this book without being convinced that there is Someone here at work besides mere human beings. Perhaps because of their very simplicity, perhaps because of their readiness to believe, to obey, to give, to suffer, and if need be to die, the Spirit of God found what he must always be seeking — a fellowship of

men and women so united in love and faith, that he can work in them and through them with the minimum of let or hindrance.[63]

Indeed it was precisely because of such a free and powerful demonstration of the Spirit of God that 'more than ever believers were added to the Lord, multitudes both of men and women'.[64] Today the climate is astonishingly similar to that facing the early Church. It is true that we have the bewildering problems created by the revolution of technology. But the apathy, the materialism, the permissive society, the fascination of the occult, the quest for meaning and significance and freedom and forgiveness and hope — all are similar. And therefore similar means for communicating the word of God are highly relevant.

A student, who was not a believer and who had previously heard and rejected the Christian faith, came to an evening service of Holy Communion in our church, when there must have been about 600 present. She had not realised that it was to be a Communion service when a friend persuaded her to come. Understandably disturbed by the service, she left halfway through; but she forgot to take her scarf with her. She returned a little later to retrieve her scarf from the front pew, and she came back into the church at the end of the administration of the bread and wine. At that point there were two prophecies: two inspired utterances, given by the Spirit of God through two members of our congregation. Although I had never personally met the girl, and she was unknown in our church, she wrote to me a few days later: 'I heard my actual thoughts in the second prophecy (something I had never heard before). I heard God actually telling me, in a church with hundreds of other people, not to run as I had done so often before... I felt and experienced God's presence — something terrifying yet wonderful.' And there and then she surrendered her life to Jesus Christ. This is almost a perfect example of Paul's words when he wrote, 'If all prophesy, and an unbeliever or outsider enters...the secrets of his heart are disclosed; and so, falling on his face, he will worship God, and declare that God is really among you'.[65]

Healing, too can be a means by which God speaks

powerfully to an individual in order to communicate his love and the truth of the gospel. I met an ex-professional boxer, who had suffered brain damage for two years and through this had been partially paralysed. Yet one day, when the poor man was trying clumsily to move an old family Bible out of the way to reach some object, God in his sovereignty suddenly gave him the gift of faith in the God of that book. Instantly he was healed. I shook his hand two days later, and he was as strong as an ox! Of course, he started to read the Bible, starting at Genesis 1, and in no time at all had come to a personal faith in Jesus Christ. This miracle of healing had prepared his heart to receive the gospel. God had spoken to him.

PRAYER AND PRAISE

We have already seen the necessity of the Holy Spirit before the written word becomes living and active. Therefore in the communicating of God's word in the early church it is not surprising to see the prominence of prayer and praise. The disciples knew that they could not begin to be effective witnesses to Christ without the power of the Spirit: not only did they lack the necessary motivation but also their preaching would have been 'in word only'. Therefore understandably they 'with one accord devoted themselves to prayer'[66] as they waited for the Spirit to fall upon them. Then came Pentecost which began, not with preaching, but with praise. Questions were asked by the crowds, partly of course because of the gift of languages, but also partly because of the reality and spontaneity of praise. Praise is a transitive verb which needs an object. We praise someone or something. Therefore when Christians are filled with praise the world will ask, What are you getting excited about? What is happening? Who or what is it that is giving you such joy? Many times I have witnessed the power of praise in the context of evangelism. In Festivals of Praise, Jesus Festivals, presentations of *Come Together,* and in other similar gatherings, there have nearly always been conversions — sometimes remarkable and outstanding ones. God has manifested himself through the praise of his people. It has always been like that. Several

times in the Old Testament, when God's people played their
instruments and raised their voices 'in praise to the Lord', we
read that 'the house of the Lord was filled with a cloud, so
that the priests could not stand to minister because of the
cloud; for the glory of the Lord filled the house of God'.[67]

Often I have witnessed something approaching this. God
has revealed his glory and spoken with power in direct
response to worship and praise. On one of many similar
occasions, during free and spontaneous singing in an Anglican service of Holy Communion (Series 3), I knew that God
had fallen upon us afresh with the power of his Spirit. One
fringe member of the congregation, who had apparently been
a backslidden Christian for many years, was restored to the
Lord and filled with his Spirit. His wife, kneeling beside him
at the Communion rails with a purely nominal faith, was
wonderfully converted and filled with the Spirit. I have seen
highly intellectual students and tough men of the world
melted to tears and brought to Christ through the power
of praise, sometimes without any preaching at all. And
Christians, too, fired with a fresh vision of the glory of
God, are released into joyful and spontaneous witness to
Christ.

All this, of course, is what we find in the Acts of the
Apostles: when the 3,000 had responded to Christ they
'devoted themselves to...the prayers'. Every day they were in
the temple and in their homes worshipping God; and as they
went on praising him, 'the Lord added to their number day
by day those who were being saved'. In Acts, Chapter 4, the
threat of persecution drove them to more praise and prayer.
They renewed their confidence in the 'Sovereign Lord'; they
praised him for his supreme control even over kings and
rulers, and, as a result, 'they were all filled with the Holy
Spirit and spoke the word of God with boldness'.[68] Later,
while the prophets and teachers of the church in Antioch
were 'worshipping the Lord and fasting', they received fresh
instructions by the Spirit for the next evangelistic thrust of
the church.[69] How many of us today recognise the importance
of worship for the guidance of God? How much easier (we
think) setting up an evangelistic sub-committee to plan the
activities of the church! And how disappointed we may

often become at the end of it all: 'Well, it was a blessing to Christians, anyway!'

PRAYERFUL RE-ORGANISATION

The Spirit of God is a Spirit of movement. He will never allow us to become static, or to fossilise into patterns and meetings which no doubt were a blessing in the past. Throughout Acts God was obviously moving and often at astonishing speed. But every now and then, such as in Acts, Chapter 6, there were problems of administration.

The evangelistic thrust of the Church was bearing remarkable fruit. Numbers were increasing daily. Soon the task of caring for the practical needs of the new disciples was beyond the energies of the apostles. The first to murmur were some Greek widows, who doubtless would have been quick to feel neglected, since the leaders of the Church were all Christian Jews. The apostles wisely put the matter before the whole Church, and seven men (all, significantly, Greek-speaking, with an obvious concern for the Greek widows) were chosen to attend to the task. The crucial point in this incident is that the apostles were in danger of being distracted from their primary task, namely 'preaching the word of God'. If this failed, everything would fail. At all costs they had to hold fast their priorities in their God-given ministry. In fact two ministries are mentioned in this passage: the ministry of the word and the ministry of 'tables' (practical and financial help). Both ministries were necessary, but for the leaders of the Church the ministry of the word was an unquestionable priority. And because they determined, at all costs, to devote themselves to prayer and preaching, the results were striking. The seven men were led into new spheres of service for Christ, which, in the two recorded cases, were astonishingly powerful. And, more than that, 'the word of God increased, and the number of the disciples multiplied greatly in Jerusalem, and a great many of the priests became obedient to the faith.'[70]

Organisation must always serve the gospel. It should lead to greater harmony amongst Christians, and set those who are thus gifted by God free to devote themselves 'to prayer and to the ministry of the word'. In far too many churches organisation does precisely the reverse: it leads to disharmony and to contentious cliques, and sidetracks those who are called to preach and teach into oiling the Machine. How many clergy, ministers and Christian workers spend the majority of their time keeping the system going!

For the sake of effective evangelism, the leadership of any church should review, at least once a year, the whole pattern of services, meetings and organisations. Ruthless questions need to be asked in an attitude of prayer and submission to God, who alone is Head of the Church. Are the meetings achieving anything *today*? Are they the best use of time and money *today*? Are they helping to build up the Body of Christ *today*? Are they assisting the Church in evangelism *today*? Are they God's best plan for *today*? Their value yesterday is not the important point. Christian work is constantly crippled by clinging to blessings and tradition of the past. God is not the God of yesterday. He is the God of today. Heaven forbid that we should continue playing religious games in one corner when the cloud and fire of God's presence have moved to another. Sometimes I speak at rallies or conventions which doubtless were times when God gloriously displayed his power yesterday. But today the word *ICHABOD* is manifestly written over the whole affair: 'the glory of the Lord has departed'.

SOCIAL ACTION AND SERVICE

The New Testament Church became famous for its practical love and social concern towards those in obvious need. In fact, its care of widows, for example, was so impressive that instructions were given for the 'enrolment of widows'[71] because so many were looking to the Church for financial support. This became, therefore, a powerful witness to the community of the practical love of Jesus Christ.

For too long the Church has been torn by the polarisation between the social gospel and the 'pure' gospel. We have already seen in this book the beautiful balance in the ministry of Jesus. He cared for the bodies and minds of men as well as their spiritual condition before God, and he taught frequently about man's social responsibilities as well as about his private life. Indeed, he gave us not only the great *commission*, to make disciples of all nations, but also the great *commandment,* that we should love our neighbours as ourselves. This is next in importance to loving God. Indeed, so as to leave us in no doubt about our interpretation of this commandment, he expounded it with his parable of the Good Samaritan. John Stott has wisely commented:

> Who is my neighbour, whom I am to love? He is neither a bodyless soul, nor a soulless body, nor a private individual divorced from a social environment. God made man a physical, spiritual and social being. My neighbour is a body-soul-in-community. I cannot therefore claim to love my neighbour if I'm really concerned for only one aspect of him, whether his soul or his body or his community.[72]

If we are forced to choose between evangelism and social action, a person's eternal well-being must be of even greater importance than his temporal needs. But too often this argument has been an excuse for opting out of a Christian's social responsibilities, where the work may be much more demanding, less glamorous and often slower in terms of results than direct evangelism. However, Jesus never saw such action as a waste of time in his brief ministry on earth. It was all an essential part of communicating the God of compassion and love.

Dr. Samuel Escobar has expressed the Christian's social concern well in this way:

> Christian service is not optional. It is not something we can do if we want to. It is the mark of the new life. 'You will know them by their fruits.' 'If you love me you will keep my commandments.' If we are in Christ, we have the spirit of service of Christ. So to discuss whether we should evangelize or promote social action is worthless. They go together. So we must not try to justify our service for our neighbour by claiming that it will 'help us' in our evangelism. God is equally interested in our service and in our evangelistic task... It is naive to affirm that all that is needed is new men in order to have a new society. Certainly every man should do whatever he is able to do to

get the transforming message of Christ to his fellow
citizens. But it is also true that it is precisely these new men
who sometimes need to transform the structures of society
so that there may be less injustice, less opportunity for man
to do evil to man, for exploitation.[73]

This, of course, was the frequent message of the Old
Testament prophets. In Isaiah, Chapter 58, for example, God
tells his people that it is not enough to seek him daily, to
delight to know his ways, to fast and to pray. 'Is not this the
fast that I choose: to loose the bonds of wickedness, to undo
the thongs of the yoke, to let the oppressed go free, and to
break every yoke? Is it not to share your bread with the
hungry, and bring the homeless poor into your house...?
Then shall your light break forth like the dawn.'

One outstanding example of love in action is in the Fourth
Ward Clinic, Houston, Texas. In a black ghetto of that city,
where 7,000 poor people are packed into huge blocks of flats,
Dr. Bob Eckert started a medical clinic in 1968. As a
Christian who wanted to show those living in the ghetto that
God loved them, Dr. Eckert knew that traditional door-
to-door evangelism would be utterly useless. Instead he set up
a medical clinic which offered free treatment. It began with a
table and a chair, three workers and four patients on the first
day. A notice in the waiting-room read: 'We are a private
non-funded clinic; a patient will receive no bill. He can pay
what he is able and inclined.' Dr. Eckert explained his aim
quite simply: 'We're not here to doctor. We are here to share
the Lord Jesus. The medical practice is something that comes
out of the love God has for people.' Often patients ask to be
prayed for, because they sense the atmosphere of God's love
in that clinic.

From those slender beginnings there are now 100 workers,
including 4 full-time and 12 part-time doctors. Some 100 to
200 are served every day. Moreover the reason why free
medical help can be offered is that about 80 of the 100
workers live in the extended households of the Church of the
Holy Redeemer. They therefore have minimal living ex-
penses, and enjoy the financial, physical and spiritual support
of those households. The clinic is not outwardly evangelistic,

but those who go there know that God is in that place, and many of them begin to experience his love and, before long, find Jesus Christ. Here, surely, is the word of God in action.

SUFFERING

In Acts, Chapter 7, we have the martyrdom of Stephen; 'and on that day a great persecution arose against the church in Jerusalem; and they were all scattered throughout the region of Judea and Samaria... Now those who were scattered went about preaching the word.'[74] Jesus had told them that they were to be his witnesses in Jerusalem and in all Judea and Samaria, and it was in fact through persecution that the word of God spread. The witnessing Church soon became the suffering Church; and although the word *martus* in New Testament times did not have the full force of 'martyr' as we know it today, towards the middle of the second century, persecution and violent death for the sake of Christ became the daily bread of the Church; and then *martus* became the technical term for the act of being a witness by the shedding of one's blood. However, even in New Testament days, witness and suffering were very closely linked.

'Witness', of course, is a favourite word, especially with Luke and John. *Martus* comes thirty-four times, *marturein* seventy-six and *marturion* twenty. The followers of Jesus were not to be surprised by the fiery ordeal coming upon them; rather, they were to rejoice in sharing the sufferings of Christ, because they were called to be witnesses to these sufferings. When Paul talked about them being ambassadors for Christ, 'God making his appeal through us', he went on to say,

> As servants of God we commend ourselves in every way: through great endurance, in afflictions, hardships, calamities, beatings, imprisonments, tumults, labours, watching, hunger... We are treated as impostors, and yet are true; as unknown, and yet well known; as dying, and behold we live; as punished, and yet not killed; as sorrowful, yet always rejoicing; as poor, yet making many rich; as having nothing, and yet possessing everything.[75]

They were called not only to believe in Christ, but also to suffer for his sake. It is frequently through suffering that God can speak powerfully. Indeed, if we are to know the 'power of his resurrection' we must also know the 'fellowship of his sufferings'. Such sufferings may not be in terms of great heroics, but in the loneliness, frustration, perplexity and afflictions that will often be experienced in tough and unglamorous situations where Christians may toil away for years, with very little outwardly to show for their labours.

Further, it is often through suffering that the Holy Spirit imprints deeply God's word in our hearts, so that later we speak that word with added authority and power. We really know, through the fires of suffering, what the word of God means.

THE POWER OF THE HOLY SPIRIT

Christ promised his disciples power when the Holy Spirit came upon them, and from Acts, Chapter 2, when the Spirit fell on them, everything started to happen. Like a stone in a pond which causes ever-widening circles to ripple out, so the Holy Spirit began this spontaneous outreach of the early Church. However, unless the Spirit is active in power, there will be little evangelism. Indeed, the means by which the word of God is increased will all be ineffective. For example, preaching without the Spirit becomes the 'dead letter', a heavy and lifeless orthodoxy; a 'church' without the warmth of the Spirit will not be united and loving; signs and wonders without the Spirit will be counterfeit — psychological or demonic; praise and prayer without the inspiration of the Spirit will be either dangerously emotional or depressingly formal; re-organisation without the guidance of the Spirit will simply be playing with structures; social action without the Spirit will be no different from that offered by an atheist: it will not convey the fragrance of Christ; suffering without the Spirit will lead to self-pity or to a self-centred persecution complex — it will not speak of Christ. Everything in evangelism depends on whether or not God has breathed his Spirit on what we are seeking to do in his name. We shall return to this crucial theme in the last chapter of this book. It is the one essential ingredient and the vital motivation which is necessary for fruitful evangelism.

NOTES

1   Mostly *logos,* though occasionally *rhema,* p. 40.
2   Acts 4:29, 31; cf. 11:19; 13:46; 14:25; 16:32, p. 40.
3   Acts 8:4, p. 40.
4   Acts 13:5; cf. 17:13, p. 40.
5   Acts 18:11, p. 40.
6   Acts 6:2, 4 (T.E.V. and R.S.V.), p. 40.
7   Acts 13:44; cf. 13:7, 19:10, p. 40.
8   Acts 8:14; 11:1; 17:11, p. 40.
9   Acts 13:48, p. 41.
10   Acts 6:7, p. 41.
11   Acts 12:24, p. 41.
12   Acts 13:49, p. 41.
13   Acts 19:20, p. 41.
14   Isaiah 55:10-11, p. 41.
15   1 Thessalonians 1:5; 2:13, p. 41.
16   1 Peter 1:23-5, p. 42.
17   Hebrews 4:12, p. 42.
18   Matthew 22:23-33, p. 42.
19   Mark 7:5-13, p. 42.
20   For further discussion on the authority of Scripture, see M. Green, *The Authority of Scripture* (Falcon), p. 42.
21   Genesis 1; Hebrew 11:3, p. 42.
22   John 1:14, p. 43.
23   Hebrews 1:1-2, p. 43.
24   Romans 1:18-20; 2:14-16, p. 43.
25   Ephesians 1:17, p. 43.
26   2 Corinthians 2:6, p. 44.
27   *Calvin* (Fontana), 156f, p. 44.
28   1 Corinthians 2:4-5, p. 44.
29   Such as those outlined in 1 Corinthians 15:1-4, p. 45.
30   Acts 4:2,8; 5:21,25,28, 42; 13:12; 15:35; 17:19; 18:11; 20:20; 28:31, p. 46.
31   Acts 5:28, p. 46.
32   Acts 2:40, for example, p. 46.
33   Acts 17:2, 17; 18:4, 19; 19:8, 9; 24:25, p. 46.
34   Acts 9:29, p. 46.
35   Acts 9:22, p.46.
36   Acts 9:22; 17:3, p. 46.
37   Acts 18:28, p. 46.
38   See Corinthians 2:15-17, p. 47.
39   Acts 17:4; 18:4; 19:8, 26; 28:23, 24, p. 47.

40   Acts 17:3, p. 47.
41   Acts 18:4, 11, p. 47.
42   Acts 19:8-10, p. 47.
43   Acts 28:23, 30-31, p. 47.
44   Acts 3:11ff.; 5:21, 42; 21:40, p. 48.
45   Acts 9:20; 13:4, 14; 14:1; 17:2, 10, 17;
      18:4, 19, 26, p. 48.
46   Acts 5:42; 10:23ff.; 16:32; 18:7, 11;
      28:23, 30f, p. 48.
47   Acts 4:5-12; 6:12, p. 48.
48   Acts 17:19, p. 48.
49   Acts 13:7, p. 48.
50   Acts 24:10, p. 48.
51   Acts 26:1ff, p. 48.
52   Acts 8:29ff, p. 48.
53   Acts 16:13; 28:23, 30, p. 48.
54   Acts 19:9, p. 48.
55   Acts 17:17, p. 48.
56   Acts 13:44, p. 49.
57   G. Kittel, *Theological Dictionary of the New
      Testament,* (Eerdmans) Vol. 7, 1073f, p. 50.
58   Acts 2:42-7, p. 50.
59   Larson, *Dare to Live Now!,* 110, quoted in
      J. R. W. Stott, *One People* (Falcon, 1969), 70, p. 51.
60   1 Corinthians 1:22f, p. 52.
61   See Romans 15:18f, p. 52
62   Acts 2:43; 3:1-10, p. 52.
63   *The Young Church in Action* (Bles), p. 52.
64   Acts 5:12-14, p. 53.
65   1 Corinthians 14:24f, p. 53.
66   Acts 1:14, p. 54.
67   2 Chronicles 5:13f, p. 55.
68   Acts 4:24-31, p. 55.
69   Acts 13:1-4, p. 55.
70   Acts 6:1-7, p. 56.
71   See 1 Timothy 5:3-10, p. 57.
72   *Walk in His Shoes* (I.V.P.), p. 58.
73   Quoted in *TEAR Times,* Autumn 1974, p. 58.
74   Acts 8:1, 4, p. 60.
75   2 Corinthians 6:4f., 8-10, p. 60.

CHAPTER FOUR

The Message of Evangelism

PAUL, WHEN WRITING to the Corinthians, reminded them of his message when he came to them preaching the gospel. It was not 'the wisdom of men' but 'the testimony of God'.[1] Other translations describe it as 'God's message', 'the attested truth of God', 'God's secret truth'. The gospel is God's revealed truth, and our primary requirement is absolute fidelity to what God has solemnly entrusted to us. Dr. J. I. Packer once wrote

> Paul, in his own estimation, was not a philosopher, not a moralist, not one of the world's wise men, but simply Christ's herald. His royal Master had given him a message to proclaim; his whole business, therefore, was to deliver that message with exact and studious faithfulness, adding nothing, altering nothing, and omitting nothing.[2]

This, after all, was the determination of Jesus himself: 'I have not spoken on my own authority; the Father who sent me has himself given me commandment what to say and what to speak. And I know that his commandment is eternal life. What I say, therefore, I say as the Father has bidden me.'[3] It is because God alone can give life, and because God's truth is always relevant, that we must be utterly faithful to the message God has given us if we are to see any spiritual life resulting from our ministry and evangelism.

1. A BIBLICAL MESSAGE

Since God has already given his word to his world, objectively in the Scriptures, our message must be first and foremost a biblical one, whatever may be the secular mood and thought of the time. To rewrite the gospel in terms which we think to be more acceptable to modern man is only to court disaster.

I once had the privilege of speaking in Oxford University on 'Christianity and Humanism' when the Humanist Society was at its zenith, boasting of a membership of 1,000. The meeting came shortly after the publication of *Honest to God,* when John Robinson rocked the ark of the Church with his radical theology. I have no doubt that Dr. Robinson was deeply and genuinely concerned to make the Christian faith more acceptable to modern man, but I could understand the comment made by the President of the Humanist Society when he spoke to me personally, after an extremely lively evening: 'Dr. Robinson thinks he has made Christians of us overnight. What in fact he has done is to prove himself an atheist like the rest of us!' Unfair, perhaps, but understandable. Although we need to explain biblical concepts in terms that really communicate, if we tamper with God's message we have thrown out the baby with the bath-water.

Within a biblical framework there are two obvious focal points.

God is Creator

Today, when the majority of people seriously question or deny the very existence of God, it is increasingly important to start at this point, and not to leap to Jesus as Saviour. There is a *Peanuts* cartoon in which Shroeder is holding up a placard saying, 'Christ is the Answer!' Behind him comes Snoopy holding up another poster, 'But what is the question?' Today we can be in danger of commercialising Christ, putting him almost on the same level as the soap powders on TV advertisements: 'This one will wash whiter all the stains in your life! Jesus will meet all your needs!'

To approach evangelism in this way is to regard man as the centre of the universe, and to encourage him to sit in judgment on Christ: 'You first satisfy my questions before I am prepared to consider believing in you!' The whole idea is hopelessly man-centred. It is not man who calls out the questions, but God. If Pilate thought that he was judging Jesus, he had yet to learn that 'at the name of Jesus every knee shall bow...and every tongue confess that Jesus Christ is Lord.'[4] Jesus is the sovereign Lord of the universe. He is the one who commands us to lay down our arms of rebellion and surrender to him. Any evangelism which soft-pedals the truth that God is Creator and Jesus is Lord is a poor short-sighted attempt to obtain quick results.

As soon as we start with God as our Creator, every part of our life matters to him; indeed every part of our life either asserts or denies the truth we are seeking to proclaim. Putting it simply, Jesus must be Lord of my home, my family, my job, my possessions, my time and my relationships. The most powerful factor about us all is not what we say, nor even what we do, but what we are. And what we really are, and what we really believe, will be eloquently expressed, one way or another, by the world we have built around us.

What sort of a God do we proclaim by our whole culture and life-style? What does the industrial society, not to mention the third world, make of the comfortable affluence of most Western Christianity? Do we really tell the world about a God who cares so much that for our sake Jesus became poor, that through his poverty we might become rich? In his book *Built as a City*, David Sheppard has many searching comments to make about the narrow concept of evangelism which concentrates on giving people gospel-words. In a profoundly important chapter on 'The Gospel for the City' (and 90 per cent of today's world are city-dwellers) he groups the mountainous problems which people face under what he calls 'four mountain ranges': personal and inter-personal problems; problems of community structures and institutions; global problems; and problems of personal destiny.[5] God's salvation is concerned with all four because they inevitably interact with one another. If Christians cling to the nuclear family unit, how can God be concerned for the overwhelming problems of loneliness which literally destroy life for millions of people today? What does that precious text mean which says that God sets the solitary into families?[6] If Christians opt out of social action, how can God relieve the oppressed? If Christians ignore politics, how can God be relevant in areas of injustice? If Christians turn a blind eye to racial tensions and inequalities, how can we say that man — any and every man — is made in the image of God, and what does it mean to proclaim that, in spite of man-made barriers, all are one in Christ Jesus?

The same need for some hard, radical thinking arises over the question of culture. Today the pace of life is fast, and the culture is changing all the time. What image of God does the Church give if our dress, music, language, style and presentation are fifty years out of date — or even twenty or ten. Is not this saying to today's world that God died yesterday; he is not the living God of today? The question we need to ask ourselves ruthlessly is this: 'What is the Spirit saying *today*?' How can we bear witness to Jesus in a culture that makes sense today? Many Christians may find it more comforting to have the songs and styles which belong to the time when God blessed them in the fifties or sixties (or even earlier!), but our task is to bear witness to the God of today and to declare that Jesus is alive today. In this tele-age people are increasingly word-resistant. It is no longer sufficient to rely on poster-texts or pulpit sermons. To give a simple illustration of this: I live in an extended family with my wife, my two children and up to seven others (the number varies from time to time). We seek to share our lives, our home, our money, our possessions, our joys and our sorrows. It is nothing to shout about and we have made many mistakes. But when we started we were told by several people in the city that they would now listen to what we were saying because of the way we were living. Our life-style, for all its faults and failings, had got through to them some truth about the living God: that he is a God who loves us and cares for us, and unites us together in Jesus Christ.

GOD IS REDEEMER

In spite of what has just been said concerning the relevance of our presentation for today, a warning should be sounded.

There is a danger of our being so 'contemporary' that we may lose the cutting-edge of the gospel. Jesus mixed freely with all sections of society: thieves, crooks, prostitutes and drop-outs. Yet he himself was utterly different, and the truth of his message was uncompromising. It was always the words given to him by his Father. It was the same, too, with the apostles. When Paul came to cosmopolitan Corinth, he found two strikingly different cultures which dominated the scene. There was the culture of the Greek, who coveted the flowery skill of oratory with all its pretence of wisdom, and there was that of the Jew, with his deeply religious traditions and his constant suspicion of anything new. Had Paul been wordly-wise, he might well have adjusted his message to this Gentile-Jewish setting. What in fact was the substance of his message? Christ crucified! 'A stumbling block to Jews and folly to Gentiles,' said Paul, but he knew that 'Jesus Christ and him crucified' was at the very heart of God's message. Moreover, it was inseparably linked with the power of God,[7] and contained the most sublime wisdom which no man could ever have discovered without the Spirit of God.[8] Paul was not concerned with the applause of men. What concerned him totally was that there should be a 'demonstration of the Spirit and power'.

What, then, was so special about this message of 'Christ and him crucified'? Certainly Paul was quite convinced that this was the heart of the matter. Later in his first letter to the Corinthians, after three detailed chapters on the gifts of the Holy Spirit, Paul went on to remind the church of the essence of the gospel. 'For I delivered to you as of first importance what I also received, that Christ died for our sins in accordance with the scriptures, that he was buried, that he was raised on the third day in accordance with the scriptures'.[9] What is so crucial about the death and resurrection of Jesus Christ? Why is this the supreme message and good news of God?

1. Our faith is historical
It is essential to anchor our faith in objective, historical events. It is not enough to say that 'Jesus gives you peace'; that is also the claim of the Guru Maharaj Ji and a host of

other prophets today. Concentrating on the purely subjective side of the Christian faith (feelings of love, joy, peace, etc.) is but one step away from confusion, deception, agnosticism or even atheism. The strength of God's message is that it is firmly rooted in the true historical events of Golgotha and the empty tomb. This is the solid foundation on which everything else rests. Today there is an increasing tendency to ignore the historical basis of the Christian faith, and to try to build a superstructure of spiritual experience. In some areas of the 'Jesus Movement', for example, there has been profound disillusionment because of the inadequate teaching on this very point. The 'Jesus trip' was fine for many thousands of young people during their spiritual honeymoon period. But when the battles and trials came, the subjective experiences began to fade, and there was no objective, historical foundation to fall back on. The whole movement therefore meant little more than the numerous other trips and experiences offered by the drug-culture of today. There have been some appalling casualties.

The New Testament Christians, however, knew that even when everything was going disastrously against them, the historical facts of Christ were the unshakeable rock, and wind and waves, storm and tempest, could make no difference at all.

> Overwhelming victory is ours through Christ who loved us enough to die for us. For I am convinced that nothing can ever separate us from his love. Death can't, and life can't. The angels won't, and all the powers of hell itself cannot keep God's love away. Our fears for today, our worries about tomorrow, or where we are — high above the sky, or in the deepest ocean — nothing will ever be able to separate us from the love of God, demonstrated by our Lord Jesus Christ when he died for us.[10]

2. The cross is central

This is unquestionably so, in the whole biblical revelation. The risen Christ rebuked the two disciples on the Emmaus road for being so slow to understand and believe 'all that the prophets have spoken'. 'Was it not necessary,' asked Jesus, 'that the Christ should suffer these things and enter into his glory?' Then he gave them a lightning study of the Old Testament Scriptures — Moses, the psalms and all the prophets. No doubt he explained that the numerous and complex levitical sacrifices merely foreshadowed the once-for-all sacrifice of the Lamb of God who had come to take away the sin of the world. No doubt he reminded them of Psalm 22 and Isaiah, Chapter 53, and many other significant passages. There are no less than fifty New Testament parallels to Isaiah, Chapter 53, showing that this chapter in particular was very much in the minds of Matthew, Mark, Luke, John, Paul and Peter.

When we turn to the New Testament, the centrality of the cross is understandably even more obvious. One third of the gospel record is taken up with the sufferings of Christ. Jesus himself called it 'his hour'; for this cause he had to come into the world; the Son of man *must* die. The first comment about Jesus made by John the Baptist concerned Christ's sacrificial offering for sin. The first topic of conversation between Moses and Elijah at the Transfiguration was the death of Christ, which he was soon to 'accomplish' (astonishing word to use!). The first thing that Jesus talked about when his disciples openly declared him to be the Son of God was his forthcoming death and resurrection.

Turning to the letters of Paul, we find that the apostle comes back to the cross time and again. For him this is the heart of the gospel: 'Far be it from me to glory except in the cross of our Lord Jesus Christ.'[11] This is remarkable! Down the centuries men and women, artists and poets, have gloried in the teaching of Christ, the humility of Christ, the compassion of Christ, the example of Christ. Why should Paul glory primarily in the ignominious death of Christ, which represented the greatest height of pain and depth of shame possible for any man, and something which Paul knew would be particularly offensive to any fellow-Jew? Indeed, since Paul had 'unceasing anguish' as he yearned for Israel to find in Jesus its Messiah, why did he choose, as central to his message, the very thing he knew would be a stumbling-block to most of them? It was, of course, because God had made Jesus to become sin for us, so that we might become right with God.[12] This is the gospel of Christ.

The writer to the Hebrews, too, is largely preoccupied with the pre-eminence of Christ and the achievement of the cross. Christ has offered for all time a single sacrifice for sins, the sacrifice of himself. Therefore we now have confidence to enter God's presence 'by the blood of Jesus'.[13] Peter, too, having protested strongly against the very idea of Christ's necessary death, and having received a stinging rebuke, took great pains to understand that event, which puzzled him more than anything else. Not surprisingly, therefore, he gives us one of the clearest statements of the cross anywhere in the Scriptures: 'Christ...died for sins once for all, the righteous for the unrighteous, that he might bring us to God.'[14] John, too, sees the blood of Jesus as the basis of all fellowship. We can have fellowship with God and with one another only when 'the blood of Jesus his Son cleanses us from all sin'.[15]

Even in the vision of heaven, recorded in Revelation, the worship by myriads of angels is centred on 'the Lamb who was slain'. This, above all, is the 'new song of heaven'.[16]

The testimony of the Church down the centuries has been the same. For 2,000 years the central service of the Church has been Holy Communion or the Lord's Supper. Here we constantly remember the death of Christ, and proclaim that death 'until he comes', for on the fact of Christ crucified rests our forgiveness for the past, our hope for the future, indeed our entire salvation. John Stott once forcefully expressed it in these words: 'If the cross is not central in our thinking, it is safe to say that our faith, whatever it be, is not the Christian faith, and our creed, whatever it be, is not the Apostles' Creed.'

The cross is not only a solid historical event, and the central theme of the Scriptures; it is also of the greatest theological significance. It is therefore not enough to speak of the crucifixion of Christ as being the greatest demonstration of the love of God we could ever have, or as being lived out today in the sufferings of mankind. The cross is linked inescapably with the sin of man, and the work that Christ accomplished there is now finished. No one word can adequately explain the meaning of the cross, but a glance at different facets of this diamond may help us to grasp the teaching of the New Testament.[17] Three concepts in particular are frequently to be found.

JUSTIFICATION

The term is borrowed from the law-courts, and the verb means 'to declare righteous'. A man who is justified may step out of that court free from guilt and without a penny to pay. He cannot be condemned again for his alleged crime in the past. The case is closed. However, the question concerning our position in the court of God is, to begin with, a very disturbing one. We are not being tried for 'alleged' sin. We are manifestly guilty. Whether we have a detailed knowledge of the law of God or not, we have turned our backs on the truth of God that could be known (through creation or conscience, if not through the Scriptures); we have rebelled against him, we have broken his laws, we have fallen far short of his standards. In Romans, Chapter 3, Paul summarises the case against us in a series of gloomy statements: 'None is righteous, no, not one; no one understands, no one seeks for God. All have turned aside, together they have gone wrong; no one does good, not even one.'[18] The whole world is guilty before God; and whether people today accept this truth, countless people suffer from a guilty conscience. Deep peace of heart and mind and conscience is exceedingly rare, except amongst those who have experienced the assurance of the forgiveness and the peace of God. What is the answer to our profound guilt before God? Only by the death of Christ: 'we are justified by his blood.'[19] Since Christ has died in our place to bear the guilt and judgment of our sin, it is possible for us, guilty though we are, to step out of the court of God free from guilt and without a penny to pay. When we trust in Christ we are declared righteous, we 'become the righteousness of God'. We cannot be condemned in the future. As far as our eternal standing before God is concerned, the case is closed; nothing can ever separate us from his love. Romans, Chapters 1-8, is a magnificent exposition of this stupendous Christian truth. Martin Luther once wrote, 'This [the truth of justification] is the truth of the gospel. It is also the principal article of all Christian doctrine, wherein the knowledge of all godliness consisteth. Most necessary it is, therefore, that we should know this article well, teach it unto others and beat it into their heads continually.'[20]

RECONCILIATION

This is a much more familiar concept in a generation which is tragically scarred by broken relationships. When two people such as husband and wife, who are meant to enjoy an unbroken relationship of love together, are in fact separated from each other, the right and natural desire is that they should be reconciled to each other. Since the essence of sin is that man goes his own way instead of God's way, thereby forsaking God, the consequence of sin is to be separated from God, or to be God-forsaken. God gives us what we choose. In his love he always ultimately respects our freedom of choice. Therefore the urgent need is for us to be reconciled to God. However, such reconciliation is exceedingly costly. In Roman law a mediator had a clear brief: he must perfectly represent both parties, and he must do everything to bring together those estranged parties, whatever the cost might be to himself. Jesus came as perfect God and perfect man, and reconciled us to God by the blood of his cross.[21] Paul, writing to the Ephesian Christians, spelt out our spiritual condition before we are made alive in Christ: 'You were dead through the trespasses and sins... You were...separated from Christ, alienated...strangers...having no hope and without God.'[22] Here is man's helpless and hopeless condition before God, brought about by his sin and rebellion. Further, since God by his very nature is vigorously opposed to all that is evil, the only way possible for reconciliation is to take away the cause of the estrangement. It was for this reason that Jesus 'appeared once for all...to put away sin by the sacrifice of himself.'[23] The barrier of sin being now removed, it is possible for man to be accepted into God's presence, when, before, this would have been totally unacceptable. Through our self-willed rebellion we had made ourselves enemies of God. But such is his love that even 'while we were enemies we were reconciled to God by the death of his Son'. Indeed it is entirely through Jesus that 'we have now received our reconciliation.'[24]

Elsewhere Paul writes, 'But now in Christ Jesus you who once were far off have been brought near in the blood of Christ...reconciled to God...through the cross.'[25] Further, since that cross is a bridge from sinful man to a holy God, God now makes his appeal to the world through his people: 'We beseech you on behalf of Christ, be reconciled to God.'[26]

REDEMPTION

The root meaning of this word is 'to set free by the payment of a price (ransom)'. The ransom, therefore, is paid as a substitute for the person held in captivity. Sadly, these ideas have become all too familiar once again in this modern world with the recent spate of kidnappings, accompanied with demands for payment before the victims can be released. Therefore this family of words is descriptive of the achievement of the cross. Man is enslaved by his own sin,[27] and cannot escape from the curse or judgment of God incurred by his sin.[28] In order to be released, therefore, a ransom must be paid, and this payment will become a substitute for the sinner who is enslaved. Some people have objected to this explanation of the cross by pressing the question: To whom is the ransom paid? To God? To the devil? However, all analogies are useful in illustrating one main truth, and it is a dangerous and misleading business to press that analogy beyond that truth. What is quite clear from the Scriptures is that Christ, by his death, paid the necessary ransom price to set us free, and that death of his was substitutionary in character: Jesus took our place and died instead of us. 'The Son of man came...to give his life as a ransom for many *(lutron anti pollon)*.'[29] 'Christ redeemed us from the curse of the law, having become a curse for *(huper)* us.'[30] 'Christ Jesus...gave himself as a ransom for all *(antilutron huper panton)*.'[31] Indeed, because that ransom has been fully paid for us by Jesus, there are two obvious consequences. In the first place, we are free to enjoy the 'glorious liberty of the children of God': free from the guilt and power of sin, and free from the righteous judgment of God. In the second place, we are no longer our own; we have been bought with a price. And instead of our self-centred existence, which leads only to slavery, we are to live to the glory of God. And that brings perfect freedom.

2. A PERSONAL MESSAGE

Unlike the philosophies of men, which can be debated and discussed with complete detachment, the message given to us by God has immediate personal implications. When Paul went to the philosophers at Athens, 'who lived there [spending] their time in nothing except telling or hearing something new', he upset many of them by bringing them a message that called for immediate and personal action: 'God commands all men everywhere to repent.'[32] God has not the slightest interest in tickling our intellectual curiosity. Instead, he is concerned with one main purpose: changing our lives and healing our relationships. Therefore the message of evangelism is personal in two ways.

First of all, *it relates to personal experience.* When Paul emphasised that the heart of the gospel was to be found in the death and resurrection of Jesus Christ, he went on immediately to underline the reality of Jesus in terms of personal experience. Certainly it was the utmost importance to stress that the Christian faith was rooted in history, in accordance with the Scriptures, and contained profound theological truths which required careful understanding. But equally important is the pragmatic test: it works! This is how I know that Jesus lives, said Paul in effect: many people have actually seen him; indeed 'he appeared also to me'. Often, in his preaching and in his writing, Paul referred to his own personal experience of Christ. Thus the authority of the preacher, evangelist or witness lies not only in the God-given message that is being proclaimed but also in the personal experience of that message. That is what Peter took pains to stress: 'For we did not follow cleverly devised myths when we make known to you the power and coming of our Lord Jesus Christ, but we were eyewitnesses of his majesty.'[33] John, writing to those who were being rocked by doubts, was even more emphatic: 'That which was from the beginning, which we have heard, which we have seen with our eyes, which we have looked upon and touched with our hands.'[34]

A. W. Tozer once wrote, 'Truth that is not experienced is

no better than error, and may be fully as dangerous. The scribes who sat in Moses' seat were not the victims of error; they were the victims of their failure to experience the truth they taught.' Today the world is looking for reality. Unless we have a clear inward experience of the living Christ, know his transforming power, and have experienced something of the joy and love of the Holy Spirit, our words, however true (as propositional statements), will strike others as pious platitudes. Sadly, so much of the preaching of today has been totally ineffective. Either we have cooked up some wishy-washy man-made substitute for the living bread from heaven — and that will not feed any hungry soul — or we have said all the right words but there was no spiritual power there, because the reality of those words had not yet been woven into our lives. If that is the case, our preaching becomes play-acting, and play-acting is the meaning of hypocrisy. David Hume, the famous philosopher and rationalist, was once seen hurrying along a street, and was asked by a friend where he was going. 'To hear Whitefield preach,' came the unexpected reply. His friend was startled. 'Surely *you* don't believe what Whitefield is preaching, do you?' 'No,' replied Hume, 'but Whitefield does!' It is this deep inward conviction, born of clear personal experience, that is essential in all true evangelism. 'Our gospel came to you not only in word, but also in power and in the Holy Spirit and with full conviction.' No wonder Paul could go on to thank God that the Thessalonians received their message 'not as the word of men but as what it really is, the word of God'. [35]

Secondly, *it calls for a response.* Jesus once warned his hearers that he had come, not to bring peace, but a sword.[36] His presence divided people. His claims were so absolute, his commands were so categorical, and his teaching came with such authority, that men and women could not remain neutral. They must be either for or against; they must say either Yes or No! Just as Jesus divided those two thieves who were crucified with him, so he has divided mankind ever since. His word always has a cutting edge, piercing through to the innermost thoughts and desires of our hearts. A response, one way or another, becomes inevitable. 'What shall we do?' they asked on the day of Pentecost. The apostolic answer could be summarised in three clear words: Repent, Believe and Receive.

REPENT

This meant a change of mind, leading to a change of heart, resulting in a change of direction. With the mind we must acknowledge our sin and guilt before God, bowing before his analysis of our spiritual and moral condition: 'The heart is deceitful above all things and desperately corrupt.'[37] However, mental assent to that is not enough; the heart must feel some sorrow and deep-seated regret that, by our sin, we have offended God and crucified his Son. Simon Peter, when he knew what he had done in denying Jesus, went out and wept bitterly. In practice, the degree of sorrow may vary considerably. Yet even the change of mind and heart is not enough. There must also be a change of direction. Repentance means an about-turn. It means being willing, with the help of Christ, to turn away from all that is wrong in our lives, and to go with Jesus instead. No man can knowingly remain disobedient to God and receive Christ at the same time. No man can hold on to sin with one hand, and try to take Jesus with the other. It simply does not work. It is interesting, moreover, that Jesus seldom left the issue with generalities. Whenever possible he pin-pointed the relevant areas involved in the command to repent. The rich young ruler had to sell all his possessions (the great idol in his life) and to give to the poor; the woman of Samaria had to sort out her abortive sex-relationships; Zacchaeus was clearly encouraged to 'restore fourfold' his dishonest gains, even though this was his own suggestion. It is seldom possible, or even wise, to spell out the full implications of discipleship, beyond the general acceptance of Jesus Christ as Lord, but often certain practical consequences of repentance will have to be faced: a young couple sleeping together must either separate or get married; dishonest business deals or fiddling the income tax returns will have to be put right as soon as possible; resentments and bitterness must be handed over immediately to Christ; racial prejudice must be confessed; pornographic literature or occult books must be destroyed. There is nothing

airy-fairy about repentance, nor is it simply a turning away
from what is wrong. It is turning towards a life of sacrificial
love, as a true follower of Jesus Christ. John the Baptist was
once asked what his baptism of repentance really meant.

> The people asked him, 'What are we to do then?' He
> answered, 'Whoever has two shirts must give one to the
> man who has none, and whoever has food must share it.'
> Some tax collectors came to be baptized and they asked
> him, 'Teacher, what are we to do?' 'Don't collect more
> than is legal,' he told them. Some soldiers also asked him,
> 'What about us? What are we to do?' He said to them,
> 'Don't take money from anyone by force or by false
> charges; be content with your pay.'[38]

BELIEVE

In the New Testament, the call to believe is a call to
discipleship. It involves a clear commitment of the will to the
person of Jesus Christ. It is far more than an intellectual
belief in the divinity of Christ or in some doctrine of the
atonement. It means a personal and total surrender to Jesus
as Saviour and Lord, with all the ethical demands involved in
such a discipleship. Indeed, in the Scriptures, faith and
obedience are joined together, and what God has joined
together, let no man put asunder. The classic example of faith
is that of Abraham: 'In hope he believed against hope, that
he should be the father of many nations; as he had been told,
"So shall your descendants be."' And although, by virtue of
the ages of Abraham and Sarah, God's promise seemed
ridiculous and impossible, 'no distrust made him waver
concerning the promise of God, but he grew strong in his
faith and he gave glory to God, fully convinced that God was
able to do what he had promised.'[39] However, it is perfectly
clear from Hebrews 11 that Abraham's faith was far more
than a pious and passive acceptance of a promise from
God. Rather it led to active and costly obedience: 'By
faith Abraham *obeyed* when he was called to go out...; and
he went out, not knowing where he was to go. By faith he so-
journed in the land of promise... By faith Abraham, when

he was tested, offered up Isaac.'[40] To believe in Jesus Christ
involves an active commitment to a person, without knowing
where he will lead you, or how he will test you. When my
wife and I were married, we both said 'I will' to each other,
promising a life-long commitment 'for better, for worse'. It
was like signing a blank cheque, and the relationship could
work only if there was a continuous total commitment of our
lives to each other. That is like what it means to believe in
Jesus Christ.

Indeed, so decisive is this belief that Jesus told his disciples
to seal it with the covenant sign of baptism. This symbolises
the essential blessings of the gospel: cleansing from sin, union
with Christ, dying to the old life, rising to the new, the gift of
the Holy Spirit, and incorporation into the Body of Christ.
Just as a bride is married into a new name, symbolising union
with her husband and entry into a new family, so the believer
is baptised 'into *(eis)* the name of the Father and of the Son
and of the Holy Spirit'.[41] It means, of course, that the believer
burns his boats. From now onwards there is no turning back.
A new life has begun.

RECEIVE

Here is an essential part of the good news: 'You shall receive
the gift of the Holy Spirit.' From the moment of commitment
to Christ, God sends the Spirit of his Son into our hearts,
crying 'Abba! Father!'[42] It is entirely through the Spirit that
we are born again into God's family. And it is through the
Spirit's continued indwelling that we enjoy the unfailing
presence of Christ in our hearts, and experience the steady
transformation of our lives into the likeness of Christ.
Without the Spirit, true Christian discipleship is an impossi-
bility: a dutiful struggling to live up to standards that are
hopelessly beyond our reach, and a futile attempt to change
the nature of our own hearts.

In popular evangelism, for many years there has been little
or no reference to the Holy Spirit at the time of conversion.
Some of the best-known evangelistic booklets, for example,
contain not a single reference to the Holy Spirit. Not only is
this a serious omission, but also it may account partly for the

confusion over the work of the Spirit subsequent to conversion. The apparent need to 'receive the Holy Spirit' at some
later date may seem a major and significant step when little
or nothing is known about the Spirit from the very beginning.
If, however, the promise and power of the Spirit is spelt out
clearly at the moment of conversion or very shortly after, the
question of a 'second' experience (of whatever label) becomes
largely irrelevant, apart from the obvious truth that a
Christian may have any number of spiritual experiences.
Certainly, at Pentecost Peter told the huge crowds that if they
repented and were baptised they would receive the gift of
the Holy Spirit, and, from their life and love and power
and praise, there is not the slightest doubt that they did
receive that gift. Of course they had to go on and on being
filled with the Spirit, but at least they knew something of the
power and liberty of the Spirit from the moment of their conversion.

Certainly there is only one way to God, and that is through
Jesus Christ, but there are numerous descriptions of that way.
Far from a rigid, doctrinaire approach, the New Testament
shows immense flexibility. Constantly Jesus adapted his
words and phrases to suit his hearers. He began where the
people were, using the thought-forms that were most meaningful to them. See how Jesus taught the immensely profound
theological truths of the gospel in terms of farming, building,
fishing, gardening, cooking, sewing, shepherding, buying and
selling. A woman came to draw water from a well, and at
once Jesus started talking about living water which could
quench her thirst for ever. How lost she would have been if he
had plunged into a sermon on justification! Some of today's
theologians want to throw away all biblical concepts on the
grounds of being 'irrelevant'. But what could be more
meaningful and relevant than explaining the gospel (according to the context and circumstances) in terms of relationships, liberation, new birth, love, life, faith, hope, peace,
forgiveness, reconciliation and justice? The disciples too, used
their common sense by preaching in terms that meant
something to their hearers. When talking with Jews,
they laced their words with scriptural quotations and allu-

sions,[43] but for the Gentiles you will find hardly any references from the Old Testament; they referred to inscriptions from heathen tombs and quotations from the Greek poets. Michael Green once summed it up like this: 'Be totally committed to the biblical Christ, and totally flexible in presentation.'

NOTES

1   1 Corinthians 2:1, p. 64.
2   *Evangelism and the Sovereignty of God* (I.V.P.), 43, p. 64.
3   John 12:49f, p. 64.
4   Philippians 2:10-11, p. 66.
5   Op. cit., Hodder & Stoughton, 331f, p. 66.
6   Psalm 68:6, p. 67.
7   See 1 Corinthians 1:17, 18, 24; 2:5, p. 68.
8   See 1 Corinthians 2:6-16, p. 68.
9   1 Corinthians 15:1-4, p. 68.
10   Romans 8:37-9 *(Living Bible)*, p. 69.
11   Galatians 6:14, p. 70.
12   2 Corinthians 5:21, p. 71.
13   Hebrews 9:26; 10:12, 19, p. 71.
14   1 Peter 3:18, p. 71.
15   1 John 1:7, p. 71.
16   See Revelation 5, p. 71.
17   For much fuller treatment see J. Denney, *The Death of Christ*, or L. Morris, *The Apostolic Preaching of the Cross* (Tyndale Press), p. 72.
18   Romans 3:10-12, p. 72.
19   Romans 3:24f.; 5:9, p. 72.
20   J. Clarke, *Commentary on the Epistle to the Galatians*, by Martin Luther, 101, p. 73.
21   See Colossians 1:20, p. 73.
22   Ephesians 2:1, 12, p. 73.
23   Hebrews 9:26, p. 73.
24   Romans 5:10f., p. 73.
25   Ephesians 2:12-16, p. 74.
26   2 Corinthians 5:20, p. 74.
27   John 8:34, p. 74.
28   Galatians 3:10, p. 74.
29   Matthew 20:28, p. 74.
30   Galatians 3:13, p. 74.
31   1 Timothy 2:5-6, p. 74.
32   Acts 17:21, 30, p. 75.
33   See 2 Peter 1:16-18, p. 75.
34   See 1 John 1:1-3, p. 75.
35   1 Thessalonians 1:5; 2:13, p. 76.

36   Matthew 10:34, p. 76.
37   Jeremiah 17:9, p. 77.
38   Luke 3:10-14 (T.E.V.), p. 78.
39   Romans 4:18-25, p. 78.
40   Hebrews 11:8-19, p. 79.
41   Matthew 28:19, p. 79.
42   Galatians 4:6; cf. Romans 8:10f, p. 79.
43   For example, Acts 2:14-36; 7:2-53, p. 80.

CHAPTER FIVE

Motives for Evangelism

IN RECENT YEARS there has been almost no end to the talk and discussion about evangelism. Conferences and congresses at every level have been held; training courses, workshops and seminars abound. Missions have been organised, counsellors trained, literature written. Yet in his stimulating book *One Way to Change the World* Leighton Ford wrote, 'It has been estimated that in spite of the combined efforts of all churches and evangelistic and missionary agencies put together it is taking 1,000 Christians an average of 365 days to win one person to Christ. This is not good enough!'[1] Why is there this gross failure of the Church to get on with its primary and urgent task of evangelism, even though the training and equipment available are better now than it has ever been? The answer is to be found in motivation. If Christians lack the desire to evangelise, then our conferences and courses, strategies and schemes, missions and crusades, will all be utterly in vain. That is a simple truth which the church has been slow to learn.

Let's face it: evangelism is not an easy task. There are many discouragements and disappointments. As an evangelist, I often think of John, Chapter 6, when a large crowd came to hear Jesus preach, partly because they were fascinated by the signs and wonders they had witnessed. On that occasion, as on many others, Jesus pulled no punches: 'Unless you eat the flesh of the Son of Man and drink his blood you can have no life in you.' Certainly what he had to offer was immensely attractive: 'I am the bread of life. Whoever comes to me shall never be hungry, and whoever believes in me shall never be thirsty.' But it was the exclusiveness and authority of his claims that made a large section of the crowd exclaim, 'This is more than we can stomach! Why listen to such words?' And John records, 'From that time on, many of his disciples withdrew and no longer went about with him.' Then, when Jesus turned to the Twelve and asked 'Do you also want to leave me?', we can hear the profound disappointment that countless Christians have subsequently experienced when there is no positive response to the gospel of Christ.

Paul, in 2 Corinthians, Chapter 4, made it clear that he knew very well the temptation to lose heart. Twice in that chapter he says 'We do not lose heart'[2]: and the repetition of this implies that he was often tempted to do so! Indeed he gives good reasons for the discouragement that many Christians have known in the realm of evangelism. In the first place there is the *spiritual blindness or apathy* that we constantly encounter. People are simply not interested; they do not want to get involved; they cannot or will not see the relevance and importance of the good news of Christ. Well, says Paul, 'even if our gospel is veiled, it is veiled only to those who are perishing. In their case the god of this world has blinded the minds of the unbelievers, to keep them from seeing the light of the gospel of the glory of Christ.' That may be the theological explanation behind the deadening apathy of so many, but if we care about the spiritual needs of people at all, few things will be more crushing or depressing than the passive indifference we encounter when we seek to bring people the most glorious truth on earth. I am never more vulnerable to attacks of depression than just after preaching or speaking to those who desperately need Christ but who remain totally unconcerned. Indeed it is for this very reason that many a Christian worker or minister has in fact lost heart, and has virtually given up the seemingly hopeless task of bringing the sceptical to a personal commitment to Christ. That is why some have effectively ceased to proclaim the New Testament gospel and have turned, as a substitute for the task of heralding Christ, to social work, counselling or teaching for their *raison d'être*.

James Stewart vividly describes the tragic picture of the disillusioned preacher:

> No longer does the zeal of God's house devour him. No longer does he mount the pulpit steps in thrilled expectancy that Jesus Christ will come amongst his folk that day, travelling in the greatness of his strength, mighty to save. Dully and drearily he speaks now about what once seemed to him the most dramatic tidings in the world. The edge and verve and passion of the message of divine forgiveness, the exultant, lyrical assurance of the presence of the risen Lord, the amazement of supernatural grace, the urge to cry 'Woe is me if I preach not the Gospel!' — all have gone. The man has lost heart. He is disillusioned. And that, for an ambassador of Christ, is tragedy.[3]

When I first moved to York I was warned by more than one Christian leader that, unless I was careful, I would lose my spiritual cutting-edge within three years. It has often been a source of comfort to remember that even Jesus wept over Jerusalem because of the blindness of the Jews to the greatest gift that God could ever offer them.

However, Paul, profoundly conscious of the astonishing privilege of being called to be a minister for Christ, said this: 'Therefore, having this ministry by the mercy of God, we do not lose heart.'[4] We go on preaching Jesus Christ as Lord. We know that God can cause light to shine out of darkness. We know that he has shone into our hearts with the light of his glory in the face of Christ. What he has done for us, he can do for anyone. Therefore we refuse to lose heart.

In the second place, however, Paul knew the crushing burden of *physical and mental tiredness* in evangelistic work. Even after a simple evangelistic service, the effort of preaching Christ and seeking to convince men about Christ has frequently left me drained and exhausted. I can think of few activities that are more demanding. Yet how many of us have known anything approaching Paul's sufferings for the gospel: beaten, stoned, shipwrecked, in constant physical danger, on frequent journeys, toil, hardships, sleepless nights, hunger and thirst, in cold and exposure? 'And apart from other things, there is the daily pressure upon me of my anxiety for all the churches. Who is weak, and I am not weak?'[5] Paul knew what it was to be afflicted, perplexed, persecuted, struck down, 'constantly facing death just as Jesus did'. And all this was endured simply for the sake of continuing to preach the gospel of Christ! If anyone might be tempted to give up through tiredness, pain or suffering, certainly Paul might have done. Yet, triumphantly he asserts: 'We do not lose heart. Though our outer nature is wasting away, our inner nature is being renewed every day. For this slight momentary affliction (!) is preparing for us an eternal weight of glory beyond all comparison.'[6]

What were the strands of motivation that gave Paul such enormous strength and persistence to go on despite the incredible pressures against him? In the second half of 2 Corinthians, Chapter 5, he mentions at least six factors which motivated his evangelistic work, all of which are focused in the person of Christ.

THE FELLOWSHIP OF CHRIST

In these two chapters Paul refers to 'we' or 'us' more than sixty times. Although he was frequently flung into lonely situations where he was forced to be on his own, Paul was profoundly convinced of the primary importance of 'partnership in the gospel'. When Jesus thrust out the seventy on their evangelistic mission he 'sent them on ahead of him, two by two'.[7] In the New Testament Church, the same principle held wherever possible. We read of Peter and John, Saul and Barnabas, Paul and Silas, Barnabas and Mark, Silas and Timothy, Paul and Luke, Paul, Silvanus and Timothy. Certainly there were times when the disciples were sent out on their own, like Philip in Samaria, or Ananias visiting Saul of Tarsus, or Peter going to Cornelius, but there is no doubt as to the importance of sharing together in the work of Christ. As the preacher in Ecclesiastes expressed it: 'Two are better than one... For if they fall, one will lift up his fellow; but woe to him who is alone when he falls and has not another to lift him up... And though a man might prevail against one who is alone, two will withstand him.'[8] Further, not only is fellowship important for prayer, encouragement and strength in the spiritual battles involved in evangelism, there is also an undoubted and powerful witness to Christ through the lives of those who are deeply committed to one another in love. Christ reveals himself not just through our individual lives as they are under the control of his Spirit but even more through our relationships with one another. Here, in some measure, however small a number, is the Body of Christ on earth. On numerous occasions I have been made aware of the presence of Christ when meeting two or more Christians whose lives are in real harmony with one another; and the impact of this is considerably greater than the sum of the individual witnesses. That is why Jesus prayed that his disciples should 'all be one' with a deep oneness that reflects the perfect love and unity of the Trinity: 'so that the world may believe that thou hast sent me'.[9] Therefore we see Paul urging the Christians at Philippi, for example, to 'stand firm in one spirit, with one mind striving side by side for the faith of the gospel'. He pleads with them to be 'of the same mind, having the same love, being in full accord and of one mind'. He entreats two women 'to agree in the Lord'.[10] There are remarkably few exhortations to evangelise in the Epistles. Instead, Paul, Peter or John spend their time urging the churches to be united in love, and to put right wrong relationships. They knew very well, following the teaching of Jesus, that warm, loving, joyful fellowship in Christ was both a powerful testimony to the reality of the living Christ and a great incentive to evangelism. Unless we go out into the world from a position of strength, supported, loved, encouraged and prayed for by other Christians, we may well get discouraged and lose heart. John Wesley used to counsel Christians, 'Remember you cannot serve him alone; you must, therefore, find companions, or make them; the Bible knows nothing of solitary religion.' Tragically, one reason for the Church's weakness in evangelism is that comparatively few local churches know the reality and warmth of Christian fellowship as described in the New Testament, and until we rediscover this, by opening our lives to the love of the Spirit of God, one of the foremost means and encouragements to evangelism will be missing. The recent rapid growth of house-churches, which often draw away some of the liveliest Christians from their own local churches, is a rebuke for the dismal failure and lack of fellowship within most traditional structures. I am not an enthusiast for the house-church movement, but in many situations I can very well understand the reasons for this development.

THE JUDGMENT OF CHRIST

'We must all appear before the judgment seat of Christ, so that each one may receive good or evil, according to what he has done in the body. Therefore, knowing the fear of the Lord, we persuade men.'[11] Why should the coming judgment of Christ be a vital and powerful factor for evangelism? In the first place, it is sobering to remember that Christians themselves will one day be judged: 'We all must appear.' On that day our work as Christians will be tested. Even though we have the rock-like foundation of Jesus Christ as the basis of future security, the 'materials' with which we have built on that foundation will be searchingly tested by fire.[12] What have we done with our lives since the time of our conversion? How have we used our time and money and energies for the work of the gospel? Have we made full use of the gifts and opportunities given to us by God? Many of the parables of Jesus make it clear that one day each of us will have to give account to God for all these things. At present we are no more than stewards of his gifts: we are 'servants of Christ and stewards of the mysteries of God' (meaning primarily the gospel). Moreover, 'it is required of stewards that they be found trustworthy'. 'And,' continues Paul, 'it is the Lord who judges.' We may be able to deceive others and to justify ourselves concerning our efforts to win people for Christ, but one day he 'will bring to light the things now hidden in darkness and will disclose the purposes of the heart'.[13] If, then, we have any concept of the seriousness of that Judgment Day, we must do all we possibly can to persuade people of the truth of Jesus Christ.

In the second place, those without Christ will be judged on that day. In Weymouth's translation, 'we all have to appear without disguise before the tribunal of Christ'. Today the extreme seriousness of man's need before God is often disguised by a comparatively decent, happy and well-meaning life. Some even believe in God; many are concerned to create a just and fair society. Their very real spiritual need is not at all obvious. But at the tribunal of Christ, the superficial mask will be stripped away, and they will be seen as they really are: 'separated from Christ...having no hope and without God'.[14] 'Mankind is divided into the righteous and the wicked with no intermediate class. There is good and evil without any middle ground. There is light and darkness without any twilight. There is heaven and hell without any purgatory. Man must choose between life and death, between being saved or lost.'[15] I am well aware that either-or statements like this are offensive to many people. But when we look for the clearest, and for that matter the strongest, teaching in the Scriptures about God's final judgment, we find it, not in the Old Testament, not in the Epistles of the New Testament, but in the words of Jesus himself. As Jeremias put it, 'The message of Jesus is not only the proclamation of salvation, but also the announcement of judgment, a cry of warning, and a call to repentance in view of the terrible urgency of the crisis. The number of parables in this category is nothing less than awe-inspiring.' Now the remarkable fact is this: Jesus, who more than anyone showed us the love of God, told us more than anyone of the judgment of God. Why? It is probably for this reason. The truths about God's judgment are so severe that we might not take them except from someone who so manifestly loved and cared. Also, in his love, he not only told us openly and frankly about our need before God, but he also did something about our need at the cost of his own blood. As he took all our sin upon himself, he made it possible for us to be forgiven and accepted by God: 'There is therefore now no condemnation for those who are in Christ Jesus.'[16] Further, the nature of love is that it risks being rejected: God in his love will never force himself upon us. The tragedy of love is when it is not returned.

In judgment God merely underlines the decision that we have made about him. Of course Jesus made it clear that the final judgment depends on our response to the opportunity and understanding that we have received, but if I do not want God, I do not have God; if I want to be on my own, on my own I shall be. That is perfectly fair, and it is the only action consistent with the love of God. The wonder of God's love is that, although we all deserve his condemnation, he offers us his mercy in Jesus Christ. If we reject his love, or neglect it (which amounts to the same thing), we have chosen the solemn alternative, which Jesus variously described as 'outer darkness', 'fire', 'torment', 'weeping and gnashing of teeth' — metaphors, no doubt, but still words deliberately chosen to describe the awful state of being totally without God and left instead to the torment of a condemning conscience and to the agonising awareness of God's displeasure. It is impossible to do justice to the gospel records without seeing the very considerable time taken by Jesus to set before us the alternatives that we face.

A clear understanding of the judgment of Christ has been one of the great motivating forces in evangelistic and missionary work. Of course, it would be better if we were spurred into action simply by the love of Christ; of course it is more honouring to Christ if men respond gladly to his love, instead of choosing him as the only alternative to judgment. But such is the love of Christ that he is willing to accept our service, or our repentance, even when it springs only out of fear of judgment. James Denney once wrote, 'Let us familiarise our minds with the fear due to Christ the Judge, and a new power will enter into our service, making it at once more urgent and more wholesome than it could otherwise be.' The opposite is equally true. Tom Allan once commented that the Church's denial of God's judgment had for years cut the nerve-cord of evangelism in Scotland. Today, in many circles the question is not so much that of calling the prodigal home as of trying to make him comfortable in his pigsty, whilst he remains still far away from home and cut off from the only person who really loves and cares.

If we grasp something of the fearful nature of God's judgment, there will be two obvious consequences. First, we shall be *urgent* in what we say. 'We persuade men,' said Paul. We don't waste our time. We use every means and God-given opportunity we have to proclaim Jesus Christ as Lord. Richard Wurmbrand, for fourteen years a religious prisoner in Romania, once made a bargain with his guards that he might preach Christ in exchange for a beating. In this way both regular services and regular beatings took place, with many committing their lives to Christ as a result.

Secondly, we shall be *consistent* in what we do: 'What we are is known to God, and I hope it is known also to your conscience.'[17] Frequently Paul linked the integrity of the messenger with the authority of the message: 'We have renounced disgraceful, underhanded ways; we refuse to practise cunning or to tamper with God's word... We put no obstacle in any one's way... You know what kind of men we proved to be among you.'[18] The consistency of our lives with the truth of the gospel is an immensely important factor in evangelism, and lack of consistency a severe hindrance. John Sung, probably the most fruitful evangelist ever known in China, was once asked about the secret of his success. Wisely he replied, 'Be careful about money. Be careful about women. And be careful to follow where God leads.' Carelessness in these three areas has frequently proved disastrous in evangelism.

THE LOVE OF CHRIST

'For the love of Christ controls us,' wrote Paul.[19] The word 'control' is an interesting word. It is used in Luke 8:45 when the multitudes surrounded and *pressed* upon Jesus. It is used in Luke 19:43 when Jesus warned Jerusalem that her enemies would *hem* her in on every side. It is most strikingly used in Luke 12:50 when Jesus said, 'I have a baptism to be baptised with; and how I am *constrained* until it is accomplished!' Here Jesus felt a powerful motivating force urging him towards the cross. He had to go that way; he had to finish the work. Paul knew something of this compulsion, too. The love of Christ pressed gently but firmly upon him; he felt surrounded and hemmed in by this love, as it contrained him in one clear direction. No matter what apathy or opposition he faced, no matter how tiring or painful the work might be, 'the love of Christ leaves us no choice' *(New English Bible* translation). How was Paul so gripped by the love of Christ? As if drawn by a magnet, he comes back to the cross: 'We are convinced that one has died for all, therefore all have died. And he died for all, that those who live might live no longer for themselves but for him who for their sake died and was raised.'[20] For Paul the cross was infinitely more than a theological statement about the atonement: Christ had died for him; Christ had suffered in his place. Paul knew, then, that he was no longer his own; he could not live any more for himself. He was bought with a price, and so he must live this glorious new life for the sake of the Son of God, who had loved him and given himself for him.

Elsewhere, Paul wrote about the love of God being poured into his heart by the Holy Spirit. This was the essence of Pentecost. As the disciples were filled with the Spirit they were released from their fears into praise, from their anxieties into powerful preaching. Again in Acts, Chapter 4, when threatened by the men responsible for the murder of Jesus, they were filled with the Spirit and spoke the word of God with boldness. And when Paul was filled with the Spirit in Acts, Chapter 9, immediately he went into the synagogues and proclaimed Jesus as the Son of God. Here was the love of Christ, manifested at the cross and poured into them by the Spirit, controlling their service and evangelism. But unless that is true, as an ever-fresh experience in our hearts, there will be little or no spontaneous witness to Christ. There may be obedience to duty, but not the natural overflow of lives that are full of the Spirit of Christ. It is out of the abundance of the heart that the mouth speaks. But if the heart is not full of the love of Christ, the mouth is unlikely to speak; or if it does speak, empty words will be uttered. John Stott once wrote, 'Nothing shuts the mouth, seals the lips, ties the tongue, like the poverty of our own spiritual experience. We do not bear witness for the simple reason that we have no witness to bear.'[21] For too long, Christian witness has been seen in terms of 'giving them the gospel'. But until we are willing to give ourselves to people in loving, sacrificial service, we have no right to give them the gospel: that is what Paul wrote to the Thessalonians. 'We were ready to share with you not only the gospel of God but also our own selves, because you had become very dear to us.'[22] Nigel Goodwin, a fine Christian actor who has demonstrated the love of Christ to so many people, once asked a group of clergy, 'Do you love people because you want to see them converted; or do you want to see them converted because you love people?'

THE POWER OF CHRIST

'If anyone is in Christ, he is a new creation: the old has passed away, behold the new has come.'[23] The Greek is even more arresting: it reads like the headlines of a newspaper. 'If anyone is in Christ — new creation!' This is the miracle of the gospel. Anyone's life can be transformed by the power of Jesus Christ. The Jewish philosopher, Martin Buber, once lamented, 'Is there any force in the world that can change that intractable thing, human nature? There's a tragedy at the heart of things.' The answer is that there is one unique force — the power of Christ. The significance of the revolution that Jesus offers is that it deals first and foremost with the heart of man. Certainly he has revolutionary things to say about our whole life-style and our attitudes towards people and possessions, friends and enemies. But to begin with he offers us a new heart and a new spirit.

From this, it follows that we should have a vision for unlikely people: 'With us therefore worldly standards have ceased to count in our estimate of any man; even if once they counted in our understanding of Christ, they do so now no longer.'[24] Hardly anyone was less likely as a candidate for Christ than Saul of Tarsus, an ardent Jew, trained as a scholar at the finest university of his time, and fanatically opposed to the followers of Jesus. Yet the startling fact remains that if *anyone* is in Christ — new creation! We need therefore to look at people in two ways. We need to love them as they are, and not as we would like them to be, and at the same time we need to see them as they could become in Christ. That was surely how Ananias approached the dreaded Saul of Tarsus: 'Brother Saul, the Lord Jesus...has sent me that you may regain your sight and be filled with the Holy Spirit.' What staggering vision Ananias had, as he obeyed the promptings of the Spirit of God!

Notice, too, that the miracle of a new creation is for those who are 'in Christ', not just in a Christian argument, nor in

the Christian religion. Paul, when he came to Corinth, longed
that his speech and message should be 'not in plausible words
of wisdom, but in demonstration of the Spirit and power, that
your faith might not rest in the wisdom of men but in the
power of God'.[25] It may often be necessary to 'persuade men'
by answering objections and by arguing the reasonableness of
the Christian Faith. But if a person's faith rests simply in a
clever argument, he is always at the mercy of what may seem
to him to be a cleverer argument. Therefore it must be our
primary concern, not to win arguments, but to lead a person
into Christ, with this faith resting firmly in the power of God.
This can happen only if the Holy Spirit is genuinely at work
in that situation, confronting that person with the living
Christ. Prayer, therefore, is essential in all true evangelistic
work in order to lift a person from the realm of argument into
the realm of faith. Only the Spirit can touch someone with
the power of God. However, it is this conviction that nothing
is too hard for the Lord, and that no person is beyond the
transforming power of Christ, which should enable us
not to lose heart when the going is tough. Of course, the
full potential of a new creation, even when that person
is genuinely 'in Christ', will not emerge overnight. We must
not be discouraged if numerous problems persist even
after conversion. At times Jesus must have almost despaired
at his disciples: they were so slow to understand, so slow to
believe, and so quick to act on impulse. When it came to
the crucial test, all the apostles failed. Yet they were still
destined to be leaders of the greatest revolution the world has
ever seen.

THE MINISTRY OF CHRIST

'All this is from God, who through Christ reconciled us to
himself and gave us the ministry of reconciliation.'[26] Before
any reconciliation can take place between two parties that
have been estranged, the cause of the separation must be
dealt with. We have already seen briefly on page 73 that Jesus
as mediator, perfectly representing both man and God,
brought man and God together by taking upon himself the
cause of separation, namely, our sin. The astonishing thing is

that, having made such a reconciliation possible, God has given to us, as a solemn trust, this ministry of reconciliation. If we are to be effective, therefore, close contact with both parties is essential. When Dr. Theodore F. Adams, a former president of the Baptist World Alliance, was ordained, his father charged him with these wise words, 'Ted, my son, keep close to God; Ted, my son, keep close to man; Ted, my son, bring God and men together.'[27] That is a simple yet magnificent summary of the ministry of reconciliation. If evangelism fails, it is often for one of two reasons. In the first place we may fail to keep close to God. Man-made plans and strategies are no substitute for total dependence on the Spirit of God, without whom all evangelism is futile. Unless we pray, God will not work; unless we are faithful to the gospel of Christ, God will not speak. Paul reminds us in this passage that God has entrusted us with the message of reconciliation, and without this God-given message there can be no effective ministry of reconciliation. We must at all costs keep close to God, trusting in his power and preaching his word. In the second place, evangelism will fail if we do not keep close to man. Again Leighton Ford makes the point well:

Christian isolationism has been a constant barrier to evangelism. Many Christians have been so afraid of being contaminated by worldliness that they have avoided any social contacts with unconverted persons. As a result, they have no natural bridges for evangelism; what witnessing they do is usually artificial and forced rather than the spontaneous outgrowth of genuine friendship... Part of Jesus' attractiveness, which drew secular people like a magnet, was his wonderful love of life, his natural appealing friendliness. Luke shows Jesus going from dinner party to dinner party, teaching the gospel to the guests. If Jesus came back today and mingled with gamblers, the skid-row crowd and the cocktail set, a lot of shocked Christians would throw up their hands and say he was too worldly![28]

It is not easy keeping the balance. Some Christians have become so wrapped in Bible studies, prayer meetings and church-based activities that they have lost all contact with the world. Others, reacting against this trap, have become so involved with the world, together with its values and way of life, that they have virtually lost all vital contact with God. In neither case can we perform the ministry of reconciliation. However, if we remember what it cost for God through Christ to reconcile us to himself, we should be profoundly thankful that he has entrusted to us the enormous privilege of bringing men and women back to God.

THE DEATH OF CHRIST

'So we are ambassadors for Christ, God making his appeal through us. We beseech you on behalf of Christ, be reconciled to God. For our sake he made him to be sin who knew no sin, so that in him we might become the righteousness of God.'[29] The cross is the final compelling motive behind all evangelism. When Jesus died at Calvary it was as though he took man in one hand and God in the other, bringing the two together by being made sin for us. These are devastating words! They speak of God pouring all the filth of our sin into Jesus so that, as Luther once expressed it, Jesus became the greatest liar, perjurer, thief, adulterer and murderer that mankind has ever known. Not that he committed these sins, but because he actually was made sin for us! Therefore, because he was 'made sin for us', God made peace with us by the blood of his cross.[30] It is not an easy thing being a peacemaker. It cost Jesus his life. It meant that he had to appropriate the filth of our sin upon himself. Thus when Jesus said 'Blessed are the peacemakers, for they shall be called sons of God', he knew that calling us into this peace-making ministry as sons of God, or ambassadors for Christ, would involve considerable sacrifice — in some cases the ultimate sacrifice of our lives. But this is the only way in which God can make his appeal through us to the world. We may be tempted to lose heart, perhaps on numerous occasions. If so, 'consider him who endured from sinners such hostility against himself, so that you may not grow weary or fainthearted.'[31] In the last analysis we must always come back to the cross of Jesus Christ.

NOTES

1   Op. cit. (Coverdale), 3, p. 83.
2   Verses 1,16, p. 84.
3   *Teach Yourself Preaching,* 19, p. 85.
4   2 Corinthians 4:1, p. 85.
5   2 Corinthians 11:23-9, p. 86.
6   2 Corinthians 4:8-18, p. 86.
7   Luke 10:1, p. 86.
8   Ecclesiastes 4:9-12, p. 86.
9   John 17:11, 21, p. 87.
10 Philippians 1:27; 2:1-2; 4:2, p. 87.
11 2 Corinthians 5:10f, p. 88.
12 1 Corinthians 3:10-15, p. 88.
13 1 Corinthians 4:1-5, p. 88.
14 Ephesians 2:12, p. 89.
15 O. J. Sanders, *What of the Unevangelised?* (O.M.F.), 10, p. 89.
16 Romans 8:1, p. 89.
17 2 Corinthians 5:11, p. 91.
18 2 Corinthians 4:2; 6:3; 1 Thessalonians 1:5, p. 91.
19 2 Corinthians 5:14, p. 91.
20 2 Corinthians 5:14f, p. 92.
21 *Motives and Methods of Evangelism* (I.V.P.), 17, p. 92.
22 1 Thessalonians 2:8, p. 92.
23 2 Corinthians 5:17, p. 93.
24 2 Corinthians 5:16 (N.E.B.), p. 93.
25 1 Corinthians 2:4-5, p. 94.
26 2 Corinthians 5:18, p. 94.
27 Quoted in L. Ford, *The Christian Persuader*
    (Hodder & Stoughton), 72f, p. 95.
28 Op. cit., 71f, p. 95.
29 2 Corinthians 5:20f, p. 96.
30 Colossians 1:20, p. 96.
31 Hebrews 12:3, p. 96.

CHAPTER SIX

Personal Evangelism

GOD LOVES PEOPLE, individual people created in his own image. Consequently, whoever they may be, each is of infinite value to him. No one can read the gospel records without being impressed by the attention Jesus gives to individuals: a thief, a prostitute, a fisherman, a blind man, a rich young ruler, a religious leader, a child, a housewife, a mother, an invalid — he cared for each one. The apostle John records only approximately twenty days in the life of Jesus, and a remarkable proportion of his narrative is taken up with Jesus dealing with individuals. In John, Chapter 4, for example, the first thirty verses record his conversation with one Samaritan woman, and only three verses speak of the subsequent revival in Samaria. Further, the parables of the lost sheep, the lost coin and the lost son (Luke, Chapter 15) all stress this one, main lesson: 'There will be more joy in heaven over one sinner who repents than over ninety-nine righteous persons who need no repentance.'

It is doubtful if any evangelism is effective without prayerful and persistent work with individuals. Impressive figures may be quoted to justify the big crusades or highly organised missions, but of those who profess faith in Christ, there is little doubt that the vast majority were prepared beforehand through personal evangelism, and it is because of the same individual attention that many more undoubtedly find Christ at some stage after the big event. Speaking specifically of student evangelism, although the same principle applies in virtually every situation, John Stott once wrote.

I have observed again and again, in different parts of the world, that the impact of a university mission varies according to the degree of contact which Christian students have with non-Christians. When, as so often has happened, Christians have withdrawn into a kind of closed, evangelical, monastic community, then, however good the organization and publicity, the impact of the mission is negligible. But when Christian students take their full part in university life, and are known and respected in the university, then their friends come to the mission and are receptive to the message.[1]

In similar vein, the broadcaster and writer David Winter, a persistent critic of the highly organised congresses on evangelism which have proliferated in recent years, once voiced this protest:

Eloquent speeches, visual aids, films, seminars and discussion groups are, after all, no substitute for the daily, unspectacular witness of the rank and file Christian. If that witness is consistent and open, then no improvement in tactics or strategy will better it as a means of winning people for Christ. If it is not, then no evangelistic programme, no matter how ambitious or sophisticated, will make the slightest impact. That is a lesson we have been slow to learn.

If the point has been overstated, it needs to be made in a generation of Christians who may be spending more time talking or writing about evangelism than actually doing it. I have been painfully aware of this during the writing of this book; my publishers have shown considerable patience while never-ending opportunities of talking to people about Jesus have made a manuscript on evangelism very difficult to produce, and deadlines quite impossible to keep!

Let us look, then, at the one who promised to make his disciples into fishers of men: the Master Fisherman, Jesus. His gentle approach to the needy Samaritan woman in John, Chapter 4, is particularly instructive.

He established contact
Some of the best opportunities for evangelism occur quite
naturally in ordinary, everyday settings: in a bus-queue, a
railway compartment, a hospital ward — anywhere! If we are
learning to live and walk in the Spirit, things will just
happen: there will be no need to force the pace. Here Jesus
was tired and thirsty, and resting at an obvious spot, by a
well, when along came this woman. Of course there were a
number of immediate difficulties to overcome. Racially, Jews
and Samaritans were not on speaking terms; socially, men
and women would never think of talking together in public
— it simply was not done; spiritually, he was the spotless Son
of God and she little more than a prostitute. We can
understand her suspicious reply when Jesus asked her for a
drink. Surely this was yet another man who was wanting her
for sex: 'How is it that you, a Jew, ask a drink of me, a woman
of Samaria?' Almost every word raised a barrier of suspicion
and mistrust. Of course Jesus knew that she would react like
this, but in his love, gently and thoughtfully putting himself
in her debt, he asked a favour, 'Give me a drink.' At least
contact had been established.

After years of personal evangelism I have come to learn in
particular two basic principles. In the first place, *opportunities
come in so far as we really want them.* If we are reluctant to share
our faith with others, however plausible our excuses may be,
opportunities will not readily come, or else we shall not see
them or take them. But if we genuinely long that others
should know the love of Jesus that we have experienced, then,
however nervous or inadequate we may feel, constant natural
situations will present themselves, and the Spirit's love within
us will overcome the obvious barriers of age, class, education,
race or culture that may exist. I have frequently been
surprised by the man or woman whom God has gifted as an
evangelist. But in spite of widely different temperaments and
personalities, it has usually been a genuine love for people,
coupled with a simple faith that God can use them, which has
given them this desire to bring others to Christ.

I remember vividly a holiday in Cornwall, when, before I
was married and had any children, my plan was to catch up

on all the books that had been piling upon my shelves. I loved reading; and since I spent most of my life counselling people, I was in no mood to open up conversations in the hotel where I was staying. Whilst praying one morning, after a number of quiet days of uninterrupted reading, I felt that God was gently rebuking me for being a silent ambassador for Christ in that hotel. 'But, Lord, I'm on holiday!' I protested in prayer. I was not at all confident, however, that my excuse carried much weight with a God whose love reached out to me even at the cost of his Son; so after a slight battle I gave in. 'All right, Lord, you win. I am willing to speak to anyone here if you will show me the way.' That day it was raining, and most of the guests sat around the lounge looking out of the window hopefully for a break in the grey clouds. Sitting near me was a particularly fine man, approximately my age, whom I had secretly envied at a distance for some days. He had everything, it seemed: a lovely wife, two delightful children, an easy manner, a strong physique and, I discovered later, a thoroughly good business with excellent financial prospects — a rich young ruler in fact. Nevertheless I had prayed for opportunities to share Christ, and in no time at all we were deep in conversation, talking that day for three hours about the most basic issues of life and death, God and man. He admitted that he had everything, except an ultimate purpose in life. Several other conversations followed in the next few days before the holiday ended. Two weeks later that man, thoughtfully on his own, gave his life to Christ. Today, a good many years later, God has done a wonderful work in him, his wife and family — all resulting from my being made to be willing to be God's servant in that hotel.

In the second place, I have learned that *most people, if not all, are basically hungry for God,* even when they show little signs of this on the surface. Jesus knew what was *in* man. Outward appearances are notoriously deceptive, and the heart of man will always be empty until filled with the one person for whom it was created. A man may deny that food exists, but he will still be physically hungry, for he is made that way, and a man may deny that God exists, but he will still be spiritually hungry, for he is made that way. 'I tell you,' said Jesus to his disciples, 'lift up your eyes, and see how the fields are already white for harvest.' Most people are much more ready for God, or much nearer God, than we might imagine.

At one evangelistic house-meeting, I felt constrained to change my prepared talk at the very last moment. I consequently fumbled over what I was trying to say; it was all rather a mess, and totally unworthy of the rather distinguished gathering in that house. Nevertheless, I ended with a personal prayer of commitment for those who were ready to invite Christ into their lives — something I rarely would think of doing in the context of a relaxed drawing-room meeting. Afterwards there was an awful embarrassing silence, and as I shuffled from foot to foot I felt sure that I had committed some unforgivable social sin. Eventually people stood up and moved around. One mature and self-assured woman came up to me; she was both angry and rude. Feeling more uncomfortable than ever, I tried to give her a gentle answer. Suddenly she stopped and said in some desperation, 'But I'm such a sinner that I'm sure God couldn't possibly love me.' She longed to know God's forgiveness and peace. A few moments later we were in another room, both on our knees, as she opened her heart to the love of Jesus. After a time I went back into the room, and almost exactly the same thing happened with another person. Two years later I discovered that several others had found Christ at the same meeting. I have given this story at some length, because on the surface, judging from the cultured and sophisticated gathering present, I would never have guessed the obvious spiritual hunger that existed in their hearts. How easily we trim our words to a man's outward appearance and not, as Jesus did, to his heart. On another occasion, a Christian student pointed out to me someone whom she called 'the toughest girl in our university'. What a reputation, poor thing! She had been free with sex, free with drugs, free with most things that lead a person into bondage and misery. When she found Christ one evening after a talk I had given, she told me that for the previous six years she had felt 'as guilty as hell'. Even this 'toughest girl in the university' was hungry for God.

In order to establish contact, therefore, we must pray for the clear leading of the Spirit. The more we rest in Jesus, the

more his love can reach out through us to anyone, at any
time, in any place. Fear of rebuff is probably our greatest
hindrance, but this really comes back to personal pride. What
does it matter if we *are* ignored or rejected? If we understand
anything of the pain and rejection that Jesus suffered, ours
will be a small price to pay in order to help others find new
life in him.

He aroused her curiosity
This was obviously more difficult, even after the initial
contact had been made. It is certainly difficult today in an
age noted for apathy and riddled with misunderstandings
and prejudices concerning the Christian faith. Jesus drew out
this woman partly through the inevitable attractive gentleness of his love, and partly through a series of semi-veiled
provocative statements. He neither quoted texts to her, nor
uncovered the jewel of the gospel before she was ready for it.
Merely hinting at something satisfying and exciting beyond
her present experience, he said, 'If you knew the gift of God,
and who it is that is saying to you "Give me a drink", you
would have asked him, and he would have given you living
water.' Her replies indicate that she was both confused and
intrigued. But her curiosity was thoroughly aroused when,
using the very terms most meaningful for this woman coming
to draw water from the well, Jesus continued, 'Everyone who
drinks of this water will thirst again, but whoever drinks of
the water that I shall give him will never thirst; the water
that I shall give him will become in him a spring of water
welling up to eternal life.' Here was a brilliant analogy of the
gospel, using totally relevant concepts for this needy woman.
Physically, it was obviously true: here she was, constantly
having to come to this well for the wearying and never-ending
task of drawing water to relieve perpetual thirst. But even
more vivid, this was a profound picture of her moral and
spiritual condition: always thirsty, always missing something,
never satisfied, empty, dry, disillusioned and often depressed.
'Sir, give me this water, that I may not thirst, nor come here
to draw.' She was still confused, but evidently curious.

How can we bring people to a point where they are asking
questions or requiring our help? Until they get to this stage it

is unlikely that they will listen to us when we try to share with
them the good news of Jesus. How can we make them curious
about Christ? Three words may help: reality, integrity and
testimony.

First, there is a great need for *reality*. In this plastic world,
where we are surrounded by imitations and satiated with
dogmas, most people are hungry for something that is real —
hungry for life. Is it real? Does it ring true in personal
experience? Where is the evidence for what you are saying?
Our lives, especially, will show the truth and falsehood of
what we are saying. Inescapably we *are* witnesses to Christ,
one way or another. We cannot help proclaiming him or
denying him by the very people we are, as well as by what we
may be able to say. D.T. Niles, at the New Delhi Assembly of
the World Council of Churches, correctly stated, 'Like Peter,
we are all in the courtyard of the judgment hall where Jesus is
on trial. He is on trial; he is being accused in the world today;
he, of his own choice, is delivered up into the hands of men.
That is why we have to speak, or share in Peter's denial.' Yet
it is our lives that speak more loudly than our words. Many
rebukes have come to Christians, no doubt well deserved:
'Christians claim that Jesus Christ is the Saviour of sinners,
but they show no more signs of being saved than anyone else,'
said a leading Hindu after years of examining the lives of
Christians. 'His disciples have to look more saved if I am to
believe in the Saviour,' wrote Nietzche.

Unquestionably, the first impact of the gospel for me, when
in a state of sophisticated unbelief, was *seeing* the reality of the
love and joy of Christ in a complete stranger. He spoke at a
meeting, and I have never remembered anything of what he
said. But without my being able to verbalise it at the time, he
radiated a sense of Christ's presence that was, for me, both
unmistakable and immensely attractive. For this reason
alone, I was curious: and because my curiosity had been
aroused, I was willing to talk, listen, think, ask questions, try
to understand, and within twenty-four hours I had committed my life to Jesus Christ. I was still incredibly ignorant of
nearly all the most fundamental truths of the Christian faith.
Owing to a thoroughly mixed religious background, I had
any number of tangled ideas to unravel in the months to

come. But I had found Christ, having tasted his reality in the life of another person.

Even more powerful, especially today when there is such a widespread breakdown in human relationships, is the corporate witness of Christians sharing together their common life in Jesus. Here, more than anywhere, can the gentle love and exuberant joy of Christ speak volumes. Two thousand years ago it was the person of Christ that was compellingly attractive, not the individual disciples with all their individual blemishes. Today, it is the Body of Christ, when deeply united in love, and not individual Christians, that can most of all make people hungry for God. There is an infectious happiness in Christians who really love one another as well as loving Christ. It is transparent, if it is real at all; this gives rise to natural opportunities of sharing of our faith in Christ with those who have seen and felt something attractive which they have not experienced before. This simple witness of the Body of Christ is not only fruitful, but it is also a form of communication in which any Christian can take part, whether or not he has special evangelistic gifts.

An Indian Christian made this significant comment:

> People are no longer converted to a doctrine. They can only be attracted to a way of life which they can see as a practical alternative to the values and assumptions of our competitive alienated materialistic society. We have been presenting Christianity (the system) and not Christ the person... We have to present to the world a living Christ, fresh, always life-giving and nourishing... Christianity is life in the Spirit and it can only be experienced in the loving, forgiving, sharing and liberating fellowship.[2]

People are also looking for *integrity*. With the rampant dishonesty in almost every section of society, including those in privileged positions of authority and leadership, the natural mind is suspicious. Paul took the trouble to stress the strong integrity of his ministry in the equally dishonest, pagan world of his day: 'We have renounced disgraceful, underhanded ways; we refuse to practise cunning or to tamper with God's word, but by the open statement of the truth we would commend ourselves to every man's conscience in the sight of God.'[3] Glaring inconsistencies, either in the lives we live or in the truth we preach, create serious stumbling-blocks, especially for thinking people. In his excellent paper at the Lausanne Congress on World Evangelisation, Os Guinness, speaking about 'Evangelism amongst Thinking People' said this:

> If Christianity is true...why does so much witnessing seem to be motivated by anything but truth, by subconscious guilt ('how many people have you witnessed to this week?'), or by unbiblical appeals ('win the world by...')? Why have Christians confused their social mores with God's absolutes and made so many of them into taboos? Why such a general denial of the arts and the particular misuse of the arts for the sake of evangelism? Why the polarization between the 'simple gospel' and the 'social gospel'? Why such concentration on minor points (such as smoking and drinking) to the virtual ignoring of major principles and issues (such as justice, mercy, violence, race, poverty)?... The way we operate speaks louder than what we say. Without the practice of truth, evangelism is in danger of becoming a giant institutional mouth, or as E. M. Forster dismissed it scornfully, 'Poor talkative little Christianity!'[4]

Os Guinness raised a host of other issues which also call into question the integrity of our message, but, when that integrity is to be found, at least in some measure, the world of today is much more likely to sit up and take notice.

One example of this is Christian involvement in politics or social justice. Roger Sainsbury, the Warden of the Mayflower Family Centre in Canning Town, London, and an ordained clergyman in the Church of England, was invited to become an alderman in the London Borough of Newham. When asked about his involvement in politics he replied:

> As a Christian I believe we must 'love our neighbour'. I see that love involves not just welfare and picking up the pieces after people have been hurt, but actively working to change a society that allows people to be hurt. For

instance, it is no use saying to an unemployed school-leaver, 'I am sorry you can't get a job', and then waiting until he perhaps gets into trouble with the police before helping. I must work to get jobs for school-leavers... Experience has shown the power to get things changed lies in the hands of politicians, and if I really want to love my neighbour I must be prepared to get politically involved... As a vicar I see that the Christian gospel means 'Good news of love and justice', and how can I speak about this if all people see around them is a lack of concern and injustice?[5]

Roger went on to stress that he saw his primary calling as a Christian minister, and that he might not seek re-election as a councillor the next time. But certainly the Church as a whole needs to care in obvious and tangible ways for a just society and a healthy environment in which individuals live and work.

A missionary from our congregation wrote about an incident in Peru which highlights this need for integrity:

On my way to deliver a Bible to someone who had asked for one, I knocked at the wrong door and was confronted by the owner of the house who, when he discovered the reason for my visit and the nature of my work, said, 'Look, that is the book of a past age. Look at Europe, at England, at North America — great places of the Bible. And where are they today? Right down, having lost all. No! Today's gospel is that of Lenin, of Mao tse Tung. We don't need the Bible. What we need is political change. When I see you walking about barefooted, with no coat on your back, then I will begin to think that there is something in your message. Our young people do not need that book [the Bible]. What they need is to learn a profession — something that will help them earn their living — but not that nonsense about the end of the world coming soon and about singing praises unendingly in a life after death. No sir! What we want is help to live here and now!'

My friend comments: 'The missionary of today has a great need for wisdom, discernment, faith and initiative as he tackles the problems which confront him in the area in which he is called to evangelise.'

Personal *testimony,* too, can make people curious to know more. This by itself could be superficial. Certainly it needs a consistent Christian life to support it, and an objective statement of the gospel to amplify it, but there is a natural interest in personal experience. Paul spoke several times of his personal encounter with the risen Christ;[6] Peter stressed his first-hand experience of the transfigured Christ — 'we were eye-witnesses of his majesty';[7] John wrote emphatically that he knew what he was talking about — 'we have heard...we have seen with our eyes...we have looked upon and touched...'[8] Such a testimony carries its own authority and conviction. Even if most people find abstract concepts hard to understand in this pragmatic age, they are interested in life, and a simple account of our own experience of Christ, although maybe not convincing to a determined sceptic, will make some interested and curious to know more.

Of course there are other means of arousing curiosity: the good use of literature, tape recordings, films, radio and TV. Also, spiritual gifts such as prophecies or healings can provoke a genuine spiritual search. But in all fruitful evangelism it is necessary to draw people from their apathy and mixed unbelief to a position of serious enquiry. It is no good answering questions that no one is asking. The skill is to get people raising issues which may previously have seemed irrelevant but which are in fact of fundamental importance.

He touched a sore spot

As soon as the Samaritan woman was sufficiently curious to begin to ask for 'this water' (although she was still confused), Jesus, in a gentle and sensitive way, touched the one area of her life which needed sorting out: 'Go, call your husband, and come here.' Here was an 'utterance of knowledge',[9] because until the tangled area of wrong relationships had been resolved — at least as far as this woman's will was concerned — there could be no further progress. 'I have no husband,' she answered with deceptive innocence. Jesus therefore replied with a directness that must have been stunning, 'You are right in saying, "I have no husband"; for you have had five husbands, and he whom you have is not your husband; this you said truly.' Why was it necessary for Jesus to be so blunt about the woman's sex-life when there were doubtless many aspects of her life which needed correction? The answer is that Jesus often pin-pointed the area of a person's life that mattered most for that person. If there could be repentance there (a change of mind and heart leading to a change of action), then all would be well; if not, that person simply could not enter the Kingdom of God: it would mean calling Jesus 'Lord, Lord' but not doing what he said. To the rich young ruler, therefore, Jesus spoke about the central issue in that man's life, his love of possessions: if he could sell all that he had and give to the poor, then he could come and follow Jesus. And to the woman of Samaria, Jesus spoke about her relationships with men; after all, as she said to her friends later, 'Come, see a man who told me *all I ever did.*' This summed up her life! Therefore, if Jesus could be Lord of that area of her life, then and then only could he become her Saviour. We cannot have a divided Christ; we cannot enjoy his friendship and forgiveness without at the same time submitting to his lordship.

In personal evangelism we may not always have the same penetrating word of knowledge concerning someone's private life, but we should certainly pray for this, since it is one of the gifts of the Spirit, and in any case we need to state clearly the cost of discipleship. Jesus never allowed compromise. Frequently he spelt out the demands of the Kingdom of God in a way that would discourage all but those who meant business. Unless a man is willing to deny himself, to take up his cross, to lose his life for the sake of the gospel, and to follow Christ, putting him unquestionably and unconditionally first, that man cannot be Christ's disciple. In our desire to evangelise, we should never cheapen the commitment involved. At the same time Jesus clearly spelt out this commitment in different ways at different times to different people. To those who were hurt and lonely, Jesus offered graciously his healing and love. But to those caught up in the excitement of seeing God's power at work, Jesus warned them that there was more in God's Kingdom than spiritual thrills. Obviously we must be sensitive to the person or persons with whom we are speaking. But whoever it is, it must be Christ first, or not at all.

He avoided a diversion

Faced with a challenge that was a little too personal and particular for comfort, the Samaritan woman did what nearly everyone does in a similar situation: she quickly changed the conversation to an impersonal and general question about religion: 'Sir, I perceive that you are a prophet. Our fathers worshipped on this mountain; and you say that in Jerusalem is the place where men ought to worship.' This was not completely irrelevant as a comment. She was, in this way, questioning Christ's authority to challenge her as he did; after all, Jews and Samaritans had lots of different ideas about religion, such as the right place of worship.

I remember talking to a student after an evangelistic service in Cambridge. I was explaining to him from the Bible the way by which he could find God. However, when it came to the crucial point at which he had to do something about it as an act of his own will, he threw in a typical diversion: 'I don't believe the Bible is the word of God.' As with the Samaritan woman, he was in effect challenging the authority of what was being said to him. Others, at the same point, have many times said to me,

'What about other religions?'
'Isn't it all a question of interpretation?'
'How can you explain all the suffering in the world?'
'What about predestination and free will?'
'I'm not sure that there is a God at all.'
'I don't believe that Jesus was the Son of God.'
'My idea of God is not the same as yours.'

In nearly every case, the same tactics are being employed. Some of these may be genuine intellectual or theological questions. They may have to be dealt with, if only briefly. But coming at a personal and challenging point in the conversation, as they nearly always do, they act, and are intended to act, as a diversion from the real issue.

I recognised what this Cambridge student was doing; so I

answered his objection by saying, 'Well I do believe the Bible to be the Word of God, and I have many reasons for believing this; but may I, for the time being, simply share with you how you *can* find Christ, if you are willing to do so?' He agreed. We talked a little more, looking up one or two verses. He did not want to pray with me there and then, so I left him with a booklet, asking him to contact me if he asked Christ into his life. Early next morning he came round to say that he had taken this vital step. I rejoiced with him, talked a little more about where to go from there, and then I suggested going over some of the reasons for believing the Bible to be God's word. 'I shouldn't bother,' he replied. 'It isn't really a problem!' That man is now an ordained minister in the Church of England, and someone whom God has used to help others to find Christ for many years.

With the Samaritan woman, Jesus gently and briefly dealt with her confusion, but brought her back to a spiritual issue: 'God is spirit, and those who worship him must worship in spirit and truth.' Certainly this was no time to get side-tracked on interesting theological issues which were not immediately relevant to this woman's urgent need.

He brought her to personal commitment

The woman had by now little resistance left, but she tried well-known delaying tactics: 'I know that Messiah is coming...when he comes, he will show us all things.' In other words, all this is very interesting, but there is no need to do anything about it yet. One day, perhaps. One day the Messiah is coming. When that happens, we shall be told what to do.

How familiar all this sounds! 'When I have passed my exams... When I've looked at other religions... When I've more time... When I've moved house... When the holidays come... When the holidays are over... When the children are older...'

Fortunately for this woman, Jesus had the final word when she tried to evade commitment until the coming of the Messiah: 'I who speak to you am he.' There was nothing more that she could say. She was face to face with the Christ. Off she went, therefore, to bring her friends and acquaintances (and she was well known in Samaria) to Jesus. She then began to taste the life, freedom and love she had always longed for.

There is always an urgency when helping individuals to find Christ. They are to seek the Lord while he may be found and to call upon him while he is near. In my experience there are certain times — probably not very many — when God is especially to be found and when Christ is very near. Each opportunity is therefore a critical time, and needs prayerful and sensitive handling. Time over again I have seen people brought to the very brink of decision, and then, for one reason or another, they have pulled away a little. All too often a hardening process begins to set in, and they never seem to get so close to the Lord again. Therefore gently and prayerfully we need to persuade an individual to make this personal commitment to Christ. Often I say, 'You will never find it easier than you will now' — which I am convinced is true. At the same time undue pressure could be disastrous, leading perhaps to a spiritual abortion. Once a person understands what to do, I usually ask some such question as, 'Would you like me to lead you in a personal prayer, which you can make your own, to help you to ask Christ into your life; or would you prefer to read something, and then take the step on your own when you feel you are ready?' The alternative is a helpful way of not forcing a person into a corner. If he wishes to read and pray on his own, I will encourage him to let me know as soon as he has done this, partly as a seal to his own personal commitment and partly because he will need much guidance and encouragement after that initial step. If he prefers to pray with me then and there, I will sometimes explain first what I am about to pray, and then, if he is happy with that, lead him in a personal prayer which he can make his own, silently or aloud, phrase by phrase, after me. I might pray a prayer like this:

'Lord Jesus Christ, I know I have sinned
and have gone my own way. I need your forgiveness.
Thank you for dying on the cross to take away my sin.
I am willing for you to be first in my life.
And I now commit my life to you.

I want you to be my Lord and Saviour,
And I ask you for the gift of your Spirit
to be with me for ever. Thank you, Lord Jesus. Amen.

The details of the prayer would depend on the way in which I have explained the gospel, but it would be along similar lines. I would then pray another prayer of thanksgiving, asking God that this new disciple of Christ might deepen his relationship with Christ, find fellowship with other Christians, a sphere of service in the world, and be filled with the Holy Spirit. One or two appropriate booklets at this stage might help to crystallise that first vital step.

In outlining my own personal approach I am claiming no special technique. There are many ways of leading a person to Christ. Also each individual must be cared for as an individual. A slick and mechanical approach will be fatal. At the same time I am convinced of the need to be simple and specific. Almost everyone is muddled, and vague generalities will help no one. I am profoundly grateful for the utter simplicity with which this commitment to Christ was explained to me, and I have sought to use the same method with others. Of course, in order to be simple it is essential to have a firm and clear grasp of the heart of the gospel. I have found a basic framework of immense value over the years, even though it may have constant variations. Certainly I must have used some similar structure many thousands of times over the last twenty years or more, and I have had the joy of seeing a steady stream of men and women, young and old, find a living relationship with Jesus Christ. Here is an example of what I have used:

Admit your need of Christ: Romans 3:23; 6:23; Isaiah 59:1f.
Believe that Christ has died for you: Isaiah 53:5f.; I Peter 2:24; 3:18
Count the cost of discipleship: Mark 8:34-8
Receive the gift of the Holy Spirit: Luke 11:13; John 1:12f.

NOTES

1   *Motives and Methods in Evangelism* (I.V.P.), 14, p. 98.
2   Quoted in the *C.M.S. Newsletter,* April 1975, p. 105.
3   2 Corinthians 4:2, *et al*, p. 106.
4   *Let the Earth hear His Voice,* 718f, p. 106.
5   Quoted in *Mayflower,* Autumn 1975, p. 106.
6   Acts 22:4-16; 26:9-18, p. 108.
7   2 Peter 1:16-18, p. 108.
8   1 John 1:1-3, p. 108.
9   1 Corinthians 12:8 — a spiritual gift by
    which knowledge, which is not ordinarily known,
    is given by the Holy Spirit, p. 108.

CHAPTER SEVEN

Growing Up

No MOTHER FINDS the birth of a child easy. Some pain is inevitable, and specialist skills are nearly always required. Yet, as every parent knows, the real and exacting work of raising children only begins at birth. Loving, feeding, clothing, training, encouraging, disciplining, teaching, correcting, understanding, counselling — the development from infancy to maturity demands all the wisdom, strength and patience we possess. Spiritually, precisely the same principles apply. To attempt to evangelise without accepting the responsibilities of growing-up is irresponsible. At best, it is to turn churches into spiritual nurseries.

In the New Testament there are few more sad admonitions than those addressed to brethren who were still 'babes in Christ'.[1] 'For though by this time you ought to be teachers, you need someone to teach you again the first principles of God's word. You need milk, not solid food; for every one who lives on milk...is a child.'[2] Jesus, too, was often saddened by the dullness and immaturity of his disciples who were slow to understand, quick to quarrel, and fumbling in their faith. And when Paul aimed at establishing churches which would stand firm against the false winds of doctrines, the pressures of persecution and the rottenness of moral decay, he knew the absolute importance of detailed and painstaking follow-up.

'I did not shrink from declaring to you anything that was profitable, and teaching you in public and from house to house... For three years I did not cease night or day to

admonish everyone with tears... Him we proclaim, warning every man and teaching every man in all wisdom, that
we may present every man mature in Christ. For this I toil,
striving with all the energy which he mightily inspires
within me... We were gently among you, like a nurse
taking care of her children. So, being affectionately desir-
ous of you, we were ready to share with you not only the
gospel of God but also our own selves.[3]

Indeed the aim of follow-up is that Christians should become
equipped 'for the work of ministry, for building up the Body
of Christ, until we all attain to the unity of the faith and of
the knowledge of the Son of God, to mature manhood, to the
measure of the stature of the fulness of Christ'.[4]

To achieve this aim a number of needs become obvious
from the study of the New Testament.

Flexibility
There is no ideal pattern; although a variety of 'systems' have
been proved useful, it is important to remember that God deals
with us as individuals, each with different and individual needs.
Immediately after my own conversion I was taken in hand by
David Sheppard (the present Bishop of Liverpool) who was also
studying at Cambridge University at that time. The two of us
met virtually every week for the best part of a year, with the
primary aim of studying carefully selected passages from the
Bible. Of course numerous other personal and intellectual
questions were raised at the same time. Humanly speaking, but
for this detailed personal tuition I would never have survived as
a Christian, or, at the very least, my spiritual growth would
have been considerably slower. As it was, within a year I had
received a clear call from God for the ordained ministry in the
Church of England and had been accepted by the Church as a
candidate for ordination. As I grew in the faith I used the same
method of follow-up with a number of other undergraduates,
and there were some obviously fruitful results. However, when I
started work as a curate in a dockyard area, working to a large
extent with dockyard apprentices from a totally different
background, I realised the foolishness of being a slave to a
system, and the absolute necessity of being flexible.

Several other convictions have also been with me over the years. First, it is a mistake to expect too much too soon. In the Corinthian Church, for example, which had been enriched in every way in Christ, there were grievous divisions and gross moral problems which would shake to the core many of our respectable churches of today. But the converts had come from a chaotic and corrupt society, and some hangover from the past was inevitable. Certainly Paul had some severe things to say to them, but he was, as always, encouraging as he gave thanks to God for the grace which had been given to them in Christ Jesus; indeed, they were 'not lacking in any spiritual gift'. Often I have talked with older Christians who have doubted the conversion of someone because of some severe moral lapse subsequent to his professed faith in Christ. But David's adultery, Job's outbursts, and Peter's denial, not to mention our own personal failings, should be a constant reminder of man's continued weakness and sinfulness and his daily dependence on the grace of God. In our judgments we must learn to be hard with ourselves and gentle with others.[5]

Secondly, it is a mistake to be over-anxious in this work of follow-up. A mother who is perpetually worried about the health of her child will not provide the best atmosphere for healthy growth. Paul once wrote to the Philippians, 'I am sure that he who began a good work in you will bring it to completion at the day of Jesus Christ.'[6] Always remember that, from first to last, it is God's work that counts; at best we are to be 'workers together with him'. A restful and prayerful confidence that God is well able to continue his work in the life of a young believer, even when the battles rage, is helpful in every way. We can see this perfectly exemplified in the gentle words with which Jesus warned Simon Peter about the greatest test he had so far faced: 'Simon, Simon, behold, Satan demanded to have you, that he might sift you like wheat, but I have prayed for you that your faith may not fail; and when you have turned again, strengthen your brethren.'[7] Although this was a realistic warning of the coming test, it was full of faith, and faith begets faith. Our fears and misgivings about a young Christian's spiritual well-being will nearly always become a negative and destructive influence in his life.

Thirdly, as a general rule, it is wise to counsel someone of the same sex, and also of approximately the same age or younger. Timothy was told to instruct the men, treating the older men as fathers and the younger as brothers, and Titus was urged to 'bid the older women to...train the young women'.[8] Emotional entanglements will not help spiritual progress.

Fourthly, never be too proud to seek the help of another Christian. If a local church is developing as a living body of Christ there should be a variety of gifts and ministries emerging all the time. We should expect, and indeed pray for, particular pastoral skills to blossom so that we can share together the needs of God's family as we grow up into Christ. I am profoundly thankful to God for the way in which he has developed in our own church, over the years, those with gifts of knowledge and wisdom, those with prophetic insight, those who understand about the healing of memories, those with some experience in a ministry of deliverance, and those with a ministry of intercession. The value of shared pastoral work cannot be overstressed, and every local church should pray for a complementary and mature expression of the gifts of the Spirit 'so that the church may be edified'.

Teaching

Even in Paul's missionary travels, he took every opportunity to teach young Christians and to strengthen them with the word of God. At Corinth, for example, 'he stayed a year and six months, teaching the word of God among them'.[9] Later, as he said farewell to the elders at Ephesus, he reminded them that 'for three years I did not cease night or day to admonish every one with tears. And now,' he added, 'I commend you to God and to the word of his grace, which is able to build you up and to give you the inheritance among all those who are sanctified.'[10] The new Testament Epistles, too, make the importance of detailed teaching perfectly clear. Practical exhortations were not considered sufficient; even to a mixed and motley bag of semi-educated believers (these were the constant jibes from the pagan world) Paul wrote a magnificent and comprehensive exposition of the gospel that has taxed the learning of theologians all down the centuries! Dorothy Sayers once said that the average layman in the Church of England is as able to meet an aggressive agnostic or atheist as a boy with a pea-shooter can meet a tank! Sadly much of our teaching of young Christians is of the pea-shooter variety: very few become equipped with 'weapons' which have 'divine power to destroy strongholds'.[11] Much more time and attention must be given to the instruction of Christians in the understanding and outworking of their faith.

For this purpose a number of methods have proved their value. In Western Christendom considerable emphasis has been placed on personal Bible study, and various study notes are available for almost all ages and abilities.[12] Certainly the heart of the Christian faith is a personal relationship with God through his Son Jesus Christ, and this relationship needs continuous deepening, partly through study and prayer. However, even with a suitable Bible-reading system, few new-born Christians are able to make much progress on their own, and regular personal counselling can be of the utmost value. Paul taught not only publicly but also from house to house, and he was willing to toil and strive with all his might in order to warn *every* man and teach *every* man so as to present *every* man mature in Christ.[13]

With many young Christians it will be valuable to arrange a weekly meeting on a one-to-one basis, giving an opportunity not only for personal and detailed instruction in the faith but also for individual needs and questions to be talked through. Basic themes can be covered over a period of time, such as Christian assurance, the power of the Holy Spirit, prayer, fellowship, witness and service, temptation and spiritual warfare, guidance, relationships. It is also important to cover some of the major doctrines of the faith, such as the nature of God, the person of Jesus Christ, the work of the Holy Spirit, the cross and the resurrection, justification by faith, the authority of Scripture, judgment and the return of Christ. A list of suggested passages which can form the basis of useful Bible study on these themes is given in the Appendix. In all such personal follow-up I have found a number of principles useful. First, pray before each session; it is often in prayer that the needs (sometimes the hidden needs) of a young Christian will be discerned. Second, do not overestimate a person's spiritual hunger; it is better to keep the sessions short than to be overpowering with long and heavy spiritual advice. It is not every baby that can sit down for a four-course meal! Third, where possible use an open Bible; it has potential power to change lives and it nourishes faith. Fourth, watch out for natural and spontaneous opportunities for teaching and counselling. Often the most valuable work can be done when out for a walk or doing a job of work together. Jesus constantly used ordinary and everyday incidents for his most effective teaching: farming, cooking, fishing, etc. It is the spontaneous drawing-out of lessons from daily life that makes Christianity into a living faith and Christ into a living Saviour. Fifth, lend a balanced diet of Christian books, booklets and articles to stimulate thought and action.

Having said all this, there is little doubt that systems of follow-up and materials for Bible reading have largely, in the West at any rate, been designed for a middle-class culture, for those who are used to the discipline of personal study and who are accustomed to thinking and acting as individuals. Indeed, because the 'private quiet time' has usually been assumed as indispensable to spiritual growth and maturity, a large section of society is left at a profound disadvantage, since the standards of 'the normal Christian life' are seen as impossibly high; and a surprising number of those from a middle-class background, who 'ought' to be able to cope, are landed with deep feelings of guilt. Mothers with small children, those under pressure and strain, those who are depressed, anxious or fearful — these and others like them can suffer from an acute sense of failure when strong and able Christian leaders place too much emphasis on private study and prayer. Certainly every Christian needs to develop a personal relationship with God, but it is a mistake to confuse the words 'personal' and 'private'. In the New Testament Church the emphasis is very largely on their corporate life together: they studied together, they prayed together, they worshipped together, they had meals together, they lived together, they suffered together.

With the increasing collapse of relationships today, resulting in a flood of loneliness and depression, the value of group
activities cannot be overstressed.

> Much human behaviour is learnt intuitively and non-
> rationally. What a person feels is more important than
> what he thinks. Behaviour is caught in community. A
> caring community of Christians, open to God and each
> other, sharing the means of grace and the Spirit's gifts, is
> the context in which believers can work out together the
> implications of their discipleship. For adolescents the
> power of the group is enormous. Materials and group work
> skills which help Christians to explore issues together are
> sorely lacking.[14]

After all, it is 'with all the saints' that we 'may have power to
comprehend...what is the breadth and length and height and
depth' of God's love and truth.[15] Small groups, therefore, are
invaluable. Ideally the members of such a group should learn
to share their lives together, which means that, although
Bible study might well be the solid basis of the group, their
corporate activities should be of a much wider variety,
including relaxation, entertainment, service, etc. A church
which encourages small groups for teaching, sharing and
fellowship, and which invests time and energy in training
wise leadership for these groups, is laying an excellent
foundation for steady growth. In fact, the research done by
the Urban Church Project,[16] for example, has shown that one
leader (vicar or pastor) can by himself never shepherd more
than 150-175 at the very most. Thus a large church with, say,
a staff of four, may see the congregation grow to as many as
600; but nearly always there is a levelling out at that number
(a maximum ratio of 150 to 1). The size of the parish, or the
density of population surrounding the church, makes not the
slightest difference. It is because the Church has placed too
much weight on the ordained ministry, to the neglect of lay
leadership, that we have to confess our failure in an urban
and industrial society. What is urgently needed is the
rediscovery of the small group, together with shared leadership and the whole Body of Christ being involved in the work

of ministry. The Methodist Class System with small groups meeting weekly under lay leadership for instruction and fellowship, was one of the most effective instruments for training in Christian discipleship for ordinary folk — a system tragically rejected by the Church of England, to its cost ever since.[17]

To quote Michael Eastman again, commenting on today's scene:

> Individuals find identity in groups. Warmth, support, spontaneity and mutual care characterize a whole range of unstructured, informal groups and in them the Bible becomes alive not in a formal, studied way but existentially, and life-relatedly. God creates community; truth lives in experience; life together is cool communication. The implications of this are obvious enough. It's nonsense to start with individual Bible reading for those who are non-readers. Some people may never understand the word in print. Other media are necessary. Instead of asking 'How do we help non-readers to read the Bible?' we need to concentrate on another question: 'How do people experience encounter with the living God in their everyday lives?'[18]

The Scripture Union has done some important work in answer to this question, and some excellent material is now available, assuming a group context. Indeed, it is the group which provides sufficient incentive for the study to continue and which makes the Word of God both living and relevant. Other forms of communication also are helpful: cassettes (and soon video-tapes), drama, dance, visual arts and music. Nor are these to be thought of as a gimmicky second-best for the superior daily Bible reading system used by disciplined and first-class Christians.

> The means used to mediate the word are less important than the absorption of truth into human personality through thought, prayer, practice and shared experience. Christian group life is essential and some Christians may encounter God only in company with other Christians. Bibles weren't

freely available for centuries and then only the educated
could read. The Chancellor of Ethiopia and two depressed
disciples received the word in flesh-and-blood terms...
Spend time together![19]

Speaking personally, having been used to fairly disciplined
Bible study for over twenty years (with considerable benefit, I
might add), and having experienced the value of group study
for almost the same length of time but at much greater depth
in the last few years, I can see how powerfully God can
communicate with individuals in a group setting. It is not just
the non-readers who need to rediscover the importance of
Christian community.

Alongside these smaller groups there is also the need for the
more formal task of 'declaring the whole counsel of God', and
those gifted by God with a clear teaching ministry must be
allowed to exercise their ministry for the benefit of the whole.
In my own church in York we have seen the value of a
mid-week parish fellowship, which the nucleus of the congregation attends, together with a number of much smaller
groups meeting in homes. This gives a balance between
teaching and sharing, worship and fellowship. Until persecution arose in Jerusalem, the members of the early Church
were 'day by day [both] attending the temple together and
breaking bread in their homes'. But, whatever else they did,
those who were added to the Church at once 'devoted
themselves to the apostles' teaching'.[20]

Fellowship
We have already touched on the necessity of fellowship for
healthy spiritual growth. A baby needs not only food but also
the warmth, love and security of a family to which he really
belongs. If the Church as a whole has failed in some measure
to give adequate teaching to its members, or if it has failed to
communicate effectively to the non-reading section of the
community, it has failed even more to create a true fellowship
in Christ. In how many churches can the outsider feel the
immediate impact of the love of Christ? How often can you
find really deep and meaningful relationships amongst those
who are called the people of God? When did an unbeliever,

entering your church, at once 'declare that God is really among you'? Is it any wonder that a young convert, attempting to join his local church, said that he felt himself to be in a 'refrigerator'? And is it surprising that, amongst Christians who have been well taught in Christian doctrine for many years, you will often find immature personalities, awkwardness in relationships, intensity of manner, inhibitions and anxieties — all of which indicate that, for all their theological ability, they have not become whole persons in Christ? Very likely the main cause of all this has been the absence of loving and open relationships which characterised the vitality of so much of the New Testament Church. Indeed, the writers of the Epistles spent much of their time urging the Christians to keep their relationships loving and open: only in this way could they become really mature and complete in Christ.

> Speaking the truth in love, we are to grow up in every way into him who is the head, into Christ... Be imitators of God, as beloved children. And walk in love, as Christ loved us... Be filled with the Spirit, addressing one another in psalms and hymns and spiritual songs... Be subject to one another out of reverence for Christ... Put on love, which binds everything together in perfect harmony.[21]

The truth is that when a person finds Christ he enters into an entirely new Kingdom, he belongs to an entirely new family. He has once for all come out of the kingdom of darkness and into the Kingdom of God's marvellous light. 'Once you were no people but now you are God's people.' The first sure sign of spiritual life is when he looks up into the face of God and cries, 'Abba! Father!' Here is the Spirit bearing witness with his spirit that he really is a child of God. But if something so radical has happened to a new believer that Jesus could call it a new birth, then to belong to a new family should also be radical: it is a *New Life, New Lifestyle.*[22] In many ways it is like a marriage. Indeed, after Paul's superb teaching on the husband-wife relationship he goes on to say, 'This is a great mystery, and I take it to mean Christ and the church.'[23] Even the strong relationship of marriage (in its ideal form) is only a pale reflection of the much stronger and eternal relationship between Christ and his Body, the Church. Therefore just as a young bride promises to 'forsake all other and to cleave only' to her bridegroom, finding in him a new centre of gravity for her emotions, her loyalties and her life, so it is with a young Christian and Christ, including the Body of Christ, the Church. The new Christian must now move his emotional centre of gravity to the family of God: 'This, essentially, is where I belong. This is my family. This is my home. These are my brothers and sisters. Here is my Lord and my Master, my Father and my God.' That is why Christ said, 'He who loves father or mother more than me is not worthy of me; and he who loves son or daughter more than me is not worthy of me.'[24] For too long the church has presented the image of a club: you can drop in when you like and be involved to the extent you wish. But that is not the New Testament picture. The Church is the Body of Christ, and we are inescapably members of it; the Church is the family of God, and this is where we belong; the Church is the building of God, and each living stone is indispensable to the whole; the Church is the army of Jesus Christ, and each soldier must satisfy the one who enlisted him. But unless a local church becomes a living fellowship in Christ, offering deep and loving relationships, these high-sounding words become no more than religious clichés.

It is in this atmosphere that young Christians will grow most rapidly. We can see, for example, the warm encouragement that radiates through Paul's letters: 'We were gentle among you, like a nurse taking care of her children... We were ready to share with you not only the gospel of God but also our own selves, because you had become very dear to us... Like a father with his children, we exhorted each one of you and encouraged you and charged you to lead a life worthy of God.' Further, because the converts in Thessalonica were born into a situation where the love of God could be felt and experienced, at any rate from Paul and his companions, Paul could write, 'You know what kind of men we proved to be among you for your sake. And you became imitators of us and of the Lord.'[25] In their lives and relationships together

was some visible demonstration of the love and reality of the
risen Lord Jesus. Later, in his second letter, as he witnessed
the same warmth of fellowship develop in that young Church,
he gave thanks to God 'because your faith is growing
abundantly, and the love of every one of you for one another
is increasing'.[26] Christian love, of course, is not primarily a
matter of the emotions; rather it is a love which gives and
serves, a love which forgives seventy times seven, a love which
is expressed in a deep and serious commitment of one life to
another, a love experienced as we lay down our lives for one
another — not necessarily involving dramatic suffering; it
may mean the humbling task of washing one another's feet.
Joyful service and generous giving — these are the foremost
marks of a live Christian fellowship. Indeed, the Greek word
for fellowship, *koinonia,* occurs mainly in the New Testament
in the context of the sharing of money and possessions. It is
something practical and costly, a reflection of the love of God
as he gave his only Son. Nothing speaks more powerfully of
the truth of the gospel than this quality of fellowship when
seen in a local church.

Worship

A. W. Tozer once made this pertinent comment: 'We are here
to be worshippers first and workers only second. We take a
convert and immediately make a worker out of him. God
never meant it to be so. God meant that a convert should
learn to be a worshipper, and after that he can learn to be a
worker. The work done by a worshipper will have eternity in
it.' True worship, of course, involves not only the sacrifice of
praise, but also the sacrifice of our bodies and possessions.[27] It
means giving God his worth with everything that we have.
However, learning to praise him with our lips (and maybe
with our bodies in movement and dance) can help us
considerably to love him with our hearts and with our lives.
And when a Christian begins to 'fall in love with God'
(beautifully expressed, for example, in the Song of Solomon)
the rest will follow. Again A. W. Tozer puts his finger on the
mark when he says, 'I am tired of being whipped into line, of
being urged to work harder, to pray more, to give more
generously when the speaker does not show me Christ.' Often

I am asked by clergy and church leaders how to encourage Christians to witness to their faith or to give generously or to serve joyfully. I know of only one answer: help that person fall in love with Christ. This was the immediate mark of the Spirit's outpouring on the day of Pentecost: the disciples were overwhelmed with the love of God and with the love of Christ. From then onwards, no matter how fierce the opposition or tough the battle, they could record that 'the love of Christ controls us'. And the first evidence of their new-found love for Christ at Pentecost was worship: they were caught up in praise, using languages given to them by the Holy Spirit to glorify God for his mighty works. Time and again I have seen that when a young Christian really begins to worship God, and learns to love him with heart and mind and soul and strength, his life will be open to God and he will be able to receive the power and gifts of the Spirit surprisingly quickly. Of course, praise without teaching and fellowship can become frothy and superficial. He will still have to learn the painful lessons of the crucifixion of self and submission to the Lordship of Christ. There are no short cuts to spiritual maturity. But the process can be speeded up, and the combination of relevant teaching, loving fellowship and heartful praise can be very powerful indeed.

Moreover it is often in the context of praise that God may speak, perhaps through a word of prophecy. Worship, therefore, prepares the heart to receive God's word, and releases the gifts of the Spirit which are given to build up and strengthen the Body of Christ. Worship also enriches our communication with God, and prayer becomes more meaningful and positive. As we learn to praise God for who he is, for his love and faithfulness and greatness and power, so our prayers and intercessions can be injected with new faith. When the disciples were in a tight spot in Acts, Chapter 4, they turned to prayer. In their united prayer, as recorded in that chapter, they spent most of the time praising God for his sovereign control over the whole earth, thanking him that even the most powerful and hated rulers could do only what his hand and his plan had predestined to take place. Then from this position of triumphant praise they went on confidently to ask for boldness to speak God's word and for signs and wonders to be given through the name of Jesus. No wonder they were all filled with the Holy Spirit and great grace was upon them all. When we learn to honour God with our worship, assuming that our praise accurately reflects the worship of our lives, God will also honour us.

Training

Jesus has given us a clear command that we should make disciples of all nations. It is not enough, therefore, to fill churches with believers, even if those believers are well taught in the truths of God's word, enjoying fellowship with God's people, and singing praises to God's glory. Something more is needed. In his stirring book *Call to Discipleship,*[28] Juan Carlos Ortiz, that colourful Argentinian pastor from Buenos Aires, outlines the three basic problems of the Church of today: 'The first is the eternal childhood of the believer. The second is the misplacement of the believer. The third is the lack of unity.' God made this clear to him as he surveyed his own church, which outwardly was a thriving concern. 'Although we were adding more and more people to the membership roll, all were remaining children, little babes who had to be taught the same things year after year... People who sing the same hymns for years, pray the same prayers for years, keep the same church structure, and need the same messages are not really growing. They are eternal children.'[29] Sadly, this is a fair comment for most of our churches today. How, then, can we train real disciples who are increasingly mature in Christ?

The first essential is to clarify our aim. Instead of being content to fill a church with new believers in Christ, it is important to see the New Testament picture of every Christian in the Body of Christ as a minister for Christ — nothing less: 'His gifts were...for the equipment of the saints for the work of ministry.'[30] 'In this way,' comments Ortiz, 'the entire church is comprised of ministers. The ministers are not a special breed of sheep coming from the seminary. They are simply believers who go on growing. Thus the purpose of the pastor is to make disciples, who make disciples, who make disciples, who make disciples.'[31] Aiming towards this ideal will involve a radical re-think for many Christians. First, there is no distinction between 'clergy' and 'laity': all priests are laymen (from *laos,* the people of God), and all laymen are priests — 'you are a royal priesthood'.[32] All too often the vicar or pastor is the bottleneck of the church: everything must pass through him or go out from him. With such a constriction it is not surprising that there is an acute shortage of gifts and ministries in most churches; they are simply not allowed to flow and develop.

Secondly, if this concept is clearly understood it makes little sense for clergy and ministers to move from church to church at regular and often frequent intervals. Again Ortiz expresses this vividly.

> Now a club can change presidents each year by election. But a church should never change pastors, because it is a family, and the pastor should be the father. Whoever heard of a family that changed fathers every other year, or of a father who ran off and left his family to take on another larger family? The father should be training his sons to take over the business. Thus it stands to reason that any young man wanting to learn about the Kingdom would turn to his pastor for instruction. Instead he leaves the church to go to Bible School, because the church is failing in its commission.[33]

If local churches really grasped this commission of making disciples, the role of Bible and theological colleges, and the ever urgent cries for 'more men for the ministry', would have to be reconsidered. Even if such a radical concept is unacceptable for many, the need to train disciples should still be manifestly obvious.

In the third place, it is the responsibility of the leaders of each local church to see that the members of that church are placed in the right position. 'Most church congregations are not a spiritual building, but a mountain of bricks.'[34] And most evangelistic activities are content to add to that pile of bricks. But it is God's intention that the living stones should be built into a spiritual house, with each Christian knowing exactly what his place and role is to be within that building: who is beside him, who is under him, and who is to be over him. Our relationships with one another and our submission to one another are of the utmost importance. And this is where the training of disciples becomes crucial.

Jesus spelt out the conditions of discipleship in forthright and startling terms: 'If any one comes to me and does not hate his own father and mother and wife and children and brothers and sisters, yes, and even his own life, he cannot be my disciple [meaning that our love for Jesus must be unquestionably and uncompromisingly first]... Whoever does not bear his own cross and come after me, cannot be my disciple... Whoever of you does not renounce all that he has cannot be my disciple.'[35] In short, all that we are and all that we possess belongs one hundred per cent to the Lord, if we are to be his disciples: that means *all* my time, and not just the hour or two I put in for meetings and services; *all* my money, and not just the proportion I have decided to allocate for the Lord's work; *all* my possessions, including my home, my car, my personal treasures — everything. Some of these things I shall be allowed to use for myself and my family, but Jesus is to be Lord of *all*. Therefore the disciple needs to renounce completely the covetous and possessive spirit which characterises so much of society today. Nothing is his; he has no rights of his own at all. It may be helpful, perhaps even necessary, to think carefully about everything that 'we possess' — bank balance, securities, furniture, valuables, hobbies, pastimes, clothes, family and friends, plans and ambitions, job or profession, the use of time and energy, gifts and abilities — and then mentally and prayerfully to hand the whole lot over to Jesus, acknowledging him to be the owner of our lives. These are the terms of Christian discipleship. And if we think this to be excessive, extreme, or fanatical, we need to remember that this was the spirit that set the early Church on fire for Christ, and this is also the spirit that makes most revolutionary groups of today so very much more effective than the twentieth-century Christian Church. If we took seriously the Lordship of Christ, learning to submit not only to him but also to one another out of reverence for Christ, the impact on the world today would be simply staggering. The principles of the Kingdom of God are not only radical, offering the world the greatest revolution ever seen, the revolution of love; they are also accompanied by the promised power of the Holy Spirit to make these principles realistic in practice. Tragically, we have interpreted these principles by the standards of church membership today. We need urgently, as disciples of Christ, to open our minds and our lives again to the meaning of true discipleship as laid down by our Master two thousand years ago. Only by accepting the full challenge of discipleship for ourselves can we ever hope to make disciples of others: 'you became imitators of us and of the Lord.'

In practice, probably the only way to work this out is to take a small group and then to give our lives to it. Jesus chose twelve, and during his amazingly short public ministry on earth, he lived with them, he spoke with them, rejoiced with them, wept with them and suffered with them; he sent them out on short missions, and taught them further when they came back; he loved them, was patient with them, rebuked them and corrected them. In every way he laid down his life for them, so that when his time came to leave them he had made disciples who could make disciples. In similar fashion Ortiz describes the transformation of his own church in Buenos Aires. He saw the need to form 'a new underground church' in his own home, that is, to work very closely with a small group whose influence would later ripple out to the rest of the congregation.

> So, I gave my life to these disciples. I served them. We went out to the country together. We lived together. We ate together. I opened my home to them. They came to sleep in my home. I went to sleep in their homes. Our wives started to meet together. We became like a family. And after 6 months, more or less — it didn't come overnight — these people were so changed... Others began to notice, and within three years the church became a true, integrated family of disciples of Christ.[36]

Similar principles have been the strength of various Christian communities, and of movements such as Evangelism Explosion, Operation Mobilisation and Youth With a Mission. Always the same lesson becomes clear: when people are not only won for Christ but also trained into whole-hearted disciples, then and then only can the Church begin to cut ice in the world today.

NOTES

1   1 Corinthians 1:1-2, p. 115.
2   Hebrews 5:12-14, p. 115.
3   Acts 20:20, 31; Colossians 1:28-9;
    1 Thessalonians 2:7-12; *et al*, p. 115.
4   Ephesians 4:12-13, p. 116.
5   See Galatians 6:1-5, p. 117.
6   Philippians 1:6, p. 117.
7   Luke 22:31f, p. 117.
8   1 Timothy 5:1f. Titus 2:2f, p. 118.
9   Acts 18:11, p. 118.
10 Acts 20:31f, p. 118.
11 2 Corinthians 10:3ff, p. 119.
12 E.g. those produced by the Scripture Union,
    47 Marylebone Lane, London W1M 6AX, p. 119.
13 Colossians 1:28f, p. 119.
14 Michael Eastman, 'Changing Ethical Standards
    among Young People', in *Frontier Youth
    Trust Review*, No. 5, p. 121.
15 Ephesians 3:18, p. 121.
16 Papers available from 19 Bosworth Road,
    Dagenham, Essex, p. 121.
17 Further comments on these small groups
    come in the next chapter, pp. 147-150, p. 122.
18 'Bible Reading and non-Bible Readers' in
    Frontier Youth Review, No. 5, p. 122.
19 Ibid., p. 122.
20 Acts 2:46, 42, p. 123.
21 Ephesians 4:15; 5:1f., 18f., 21; Colossians 3:14, p. 124.
22 The title of Michael Green's excellent book
    on follow-up, pub. Hodder & Stoughton, p. 124.
23 Ephesians 5:32, p. 124.
24 Matthew 10:37, p. 125.
25 1 Thessalonians 2:7-17; 1:5f, p. 125.
26 2 Thessalonians 1:3, p. 126.
27 Hebrews 13:15f.; Romans 12:1. See Chapter 9
    where the place of worship in evangelism is
    developed more fully, p. 126.
28 Published by Logos, p. 128.
29 Op. cit., 3f, p. 128.
30 Ephesians 4:11f, p. 128.
31 Op. cit., 18, p. 128.
32 1 Peter 2:9, p. 129.

33 Op. cit., 23, p. 129.
34 Op. cit., 26, p. 129.
35 Luke 14:26-33, p. 130.
36 Op. cit., 77f, p. 131.

CHAPTER EIGHT

Evangelism and the Local Church

IN HIS PAPER to the Lausanne Congress, Howard Snyder, the
Dean of the Free Methodist Theological Seminary in Sao
Paulo, said this: 'The Church is the only divinely-appointed
means for spreading the gospel... Further, evangelism makes
little sense, divorced from the fact of the Christian community... The evangelistic call intends to call persons to the Body
of Christ — the community of believers, with Jesus Christ as
its essential and sovereign head.' Certainly evangelism should
flow from every live and healthy local church. Indeed, one of
the striking features of the New Testament is that there are
very few appeals to evangelise made by the apostles to the
various churches. The great commission given by Christ is
unmistakable, of course, but in some respects it is the spiritual
equivalent to God's command in Genesis 1:28, 'Be fruitful
and multiply; and fill the earth and subdue it.' Most people
do not need constant exhortations to be fruitful and multiply;
indeed with the present population explosion the reverse is
the case! In the same way there should be a natural and
spontaneous evangelism explosion issuing from healthy
church life. 'In the apostolic Church, evangelism was some-
how "assumed" and it functioned without special techniques
or special programmes. Evangelism happened! Issuing effort-
lessly from the community of believers as light from the sun,
it was automatic, spontaneous, continuous, contagious.'[1] In
many ways church missions and evangelistic crusades are
God's second-best: if every local church were truly alive with
the Spirit of God there would be no need for the considerable

time, money and energy expended on these special events. Although the message of evangelism is always Christ, the purpose and agent of evangelism is the Church.

God is concerned, not only with personal salvation and the training of individual disciples, but also with the establishing of his Kingdom on earth. He wants us to become a new society, a living community that will demonstrate, by its new life-style, new values and new relationships, what his purpose is for the world. His original plan and ultimate aim is that those whom he has created in his own image should become a community of love. When, therefore, an individual commits his life to Jesus Christ, it is equally important that he commits his life to the Church. This is part of the significance of baptism. When Peter told the crowds at Pentecost to repent and be baptised, he intended that the outward sign should symbolise not only cleansing from sin, dying and rising again to a new life, and the gift of the Holy Spirit, but also incorporation into the Church. At any rate they got the message: at once they devoted themselves to the apostles' teaching and fellowship, and the Lord added to the Church day by day those who were being saved. If we fail to build individuals into the corporate life of the Church we have missed the purpose of evangelism.

The Church is also God's agent in evangelism. We have already seen that when Paul uses the phrase 'the Body of Christ' the world 'Body' refers, in part, to the means of communication. It is through his Body, the Church, that Christ communicates himself to the world. The word of God is not meant to be a disembodied statement of doctrinal propositions; it has to become flesh for every generation in every place. It is therefore of the utmost importance that the Church, as seen by others, is relevant to the cultural and social setting of the day, otherwise it will effectively negate the message that is being preached. During his earthly ministry Jesus was, in his person and in his teaching, disturbingly radical but at the same time intensely relevant. How, then, can the Church become relevant, and stay relevant, in a world that is changing at an ever-increasing speed? The cultural life of the younger generation, for example, changes completely about every four or five years. Moreover, as Alvin Toffler has vividly described in *Future Shock*, many people find themselves quite unable to adjust to this speed of change, and consequently lapse into apathy, loneliness, frustration, depression or despair. If the Church, then, remains primarily an institution, comparatively rigid in structure, unbending in worship, fixed in its patterns of ministry, fellowship, organisation and service, it will never begin to speak to today's world. Indeed, if you try to bend something that is rigid you will only break it. Tragically we witness today a number of broken congregations and broken clergy who have lost their relevance and are confused as to their role in a society which does not seem to need them or want them. Adding to the bewilderment is the time-consuming and desperately slow business of trying to reform the structures of the Church, with endless reports and commissions, new methods of government, new patterns of ministry, new forms of service. The intention is good, but the speed at which the Church is changing is very much slower than the speed at which the gap between the Church and the world is expanding. Mincing no words, David Winter once wrote, 'In the institutional, moribund, introverted ranks of our Christian Churches, we have a private dialogue with ourselves while man plunges suicidally on into absurdity and despair.'

The Spirit of God, however, is the Spirit of movement. If the Church is open to the continuous spiritual renewal as intended by God, it must become a living and flexible Body of Christ instead of an inflexible institution which is so crippling to evangelism. Therefore, believing that God is the Lord of the whole earth, we need to discern what his Spirit is saying and doing in the world as well as in the Church. It would be wrong to dismiss lightly the traditions of the past; but we need to ask, what *is* relevant in today's world? How can the Church be God's effective agent in evangelism, God's new society that has a prophetic and redeeming role in the world as it now exists? We cannot afford to fight yesterday's battles, still less to use yesterday's methods to fight today's battles.

1. NEW RELATIONSHIPS

Probably the most important factor in the witness of a local church is the quality of its corporate life in Christ. Unless a church can proclaim the living Christ, as seen in the united and loving relationships between its members, it has nothing to say apart from empty words and barren theology. The essence of the gospel is new relationships: in Christ all barriers are broken down — we have access to the very presence of God himself, and, regardless of culture or class, we are all one in Christ Jesus. Christ, who is our peace, has come to 'reconcile us...to God in one body through the cross'.[2] The Church which proclaims that truth must also demonstrate in a living Christian community that these barriers really have been broken down, otherwise the message is meaningless. That is no doubt why Paul, for example, took up so much space in his letters telling the Christians to keep their relationships right. Only in this way could they effectively shine as lights in the world. This, for him, was far more basic and necessary than constant calls to evangelise.

The minister of a church in a tough and difficult parish was criticised when he told a friend that his church had no active evangelistic programme. They were concentrating much more at that time on strengthening the relationships amongst the Christians. He was warned that the church would become inward-looking and die. He replied, 'Yet our concentration on building up the body and letting the Holy Spirit sort us out has added more to the church in a year than I can remember in many previous years. I believe evangelism will keep flowing only from a healthy body.'[3] Not only will such a body of believers authenticate the truth of the gospel; by being in the secure context of loving relationships, the Christians will also be much more willing and able to move as the Spirit moves, in order to remain fresh and relevant as God's living word in the society in which he has placed them.

The first-century Christians astonished the world by their outstanding generosity, even though many of them were desperately poor: by their practical care of widows and orphans, the sick and the infirm; by their loving concern for prisoners, slaves, the hungry and the oppressed; by their

generous hospitality to Christian travellers. They were known
for their sexual purity, for their hatred of cruelty and
injustice, for their obedience to civic authorities and for their
good citizenship. They were sorrowful, yet always rejoicing;
they were poor, yet they made many rich; they had nothing,
and yet they possessed everything. Here was the Spirit of
Christ speaking volumes through the united witness of God's
people. Today there are countless people with little or no
sense of belonging: they are lonely and lost, searching for
significance, and confused in a world that is falling apart. In
this situation the Church will be highly relevant if, and only
if, it becomes a genuine caring community of love. One
young person, who found the living Christ purely through the
love of very ordinary Christians surrounding her, told me,
'All my life I've wanted to be wanted.' She had been
unimpressed by the religion that had been offered to her for
many years; she would not have listened to gospel words, and
would not have read, through sheer lack of interest, an
evangelistic book. But when she found herself surrounded by
a small group of Christians who loved her and who loved one
another in their love for the Lord Jesus, she knew that she
had come home. A simple explanation of the way to Christ
was hardly necessary, apart from helping her to understand
what she had already experienced.

Such deep relationships are, of course, not easy to achieve
nor to maintain. We have to make love our aim; we have to
seek peace and pursue it.[4] Behind it all lies a deep commitment: we must learn to be as committed to one another as we
are to Christ. We must be willing to serve one another and lay
down our lives for one another. It means the sharing, not only
of our money and possessions, but also of ourselves — which
is more costly. Christian love is in no way based on
self-interest, nor is it based on feelings or emotions; it is based
on a decision. 'This doesn't mean that Christian love is rigid
or joyless, something that we must grit our teeth and plunge
into. Faithfulness and determination are essential, but it is
from this committed love that joy and affection blossom forth
in our relationships. The world expects to build lasting
relationships on emotions or self-interest — a shaky foundation. The Lord teaches us to lay down our lives for one

another unreservedly: joy and affection follow.'[5] Any church which desires to communicate the life of the risen Lord must concentrate on deepening the relationships within its fellowship.

2. NEW PRESENTATIONS

The essential message of the gospel is a fixed deposit of truth which has been solemnly entrusted to us, and therefore is never to be changed. 'Follow the pattern of the sound words which you have heard from me,' counselled the apostle Paul to young Timothy. 'Guard the truth that has been entrusted to you by the Holy Spirit who dwells within us.'[6] However, the presentation of this truth can, and must, vary from age to age. This is the age of apathy when most people are not asking questions about God or about the Christian faith; and when no questions are being asked, it is useless attempting to give the answers. Nor should we, in our attempt to be relevant in our communication, simply ape the fashions of the world. Certainly we must study the methods of communication which are effective for today. But, believing in the creative (and not imitative) Spirit of God, we should look for and expect fresh and creative expressions of the living Christ which are relevant for today, and yet which may be entirely different from what the world is saying and from the way it is saying it.

One illustration of this is the renewed interest in the arts as an expression of the Christian faith: drama, dance, mime, poetry, crafts, and of course music and singing. Some people, admittedly, have been cautious or openly critical of this development. For them, the supreme authority of Scripture permits the imitation of New Testament methods *only*. Where, it is asked, is there any evidence of dance or mime in the New Testament? The argument often lays heavy stress on the conviction that, since the coming of Christ, God has blessed only one means of communication for the salvation of men, namely the preaching of his word. Thus all other attempted forms of communication detract from the preaching ministry, weaken the authority of Scripture, and lessen the desire for personal Bible study. They are no more than carnal forms of 'Christian' entertainment.

In answer to this serious criticism, the Bible makes it clear that down the centuries God has spoken in many and various ways, and his actions have been just as vital a part of his revelation as his words. Further, on what grounds are we to limit ourselves to New Testament methods alone? Jesus himself constantly drew his critics' attention to the authority and example of the Old Testament Scriptures, and there we find Ezekiel, for instance, a master of street theatre, with prophetic and symbolic mime or drama forming an integral part of his God-given ministry. Moreover, to restrict Christian communication today to the methods of the New Testament is surely to limit the sovereignty of Christ. Being Lord of all, he is Lord of culture, and, in his sovereignty, he would surely want to guide us in every age and in every culture to the appropriate presentation of the unchanging message of the gospel. Indeed, even the New Testament methods of communication between God and man are considerably varied. With the incarnation, the Word was made flesh: nothing could have been more powerful and dramatic than this, but it was not verbal preaching. And, as we have seen in Chapter 2, in the ministry of Jesus proclamation and demonstration went hand in hand. He used parables, visual aids (a child set in the midst of the disciples, a coin in a fish's mouth), and of course signs and wonders. Paul, too, declared that it was 'by word and deed, by the power of signs and wonders, by the power of the Holy Spirit'[7] that God had given him such a fruitful ministry amongst the Gentiles. Various spiritual gifts, especially prophecy, became a vital part of God speaking to his people. And some of these prophecies were in dramatic form: when Agabus came to Paul 'he took Paul's girdle and bound his own feet and hands, and said, "Thus says the Holy Spirit, 'So shall the Jews at Jerusalem bind the man who owns this girdle and deliver him into the hands of the Gentiles.'"[8] Paul himself was converted, not through preaching, but through a direct encounter with the risen Christ, although a number of other factors, such as the martyrdom of Stephen, no doubt prepared the way for him.

In an age when people are satiated with words, various art

forms can be immensely effective, at least in the first stages of communication. Let me give one illustration of this from the standpoint of a local church. In the church I serve in York, small singing and dancing groups have formed, and have become expressions of our life and worship together. As we are in a privileged position at the centre of a famous tourist city, and stand adjacent to the largest and perhaps finest Gothic building in Europe, York Minster, we are surrounded by numerous visitors from all over the world. During the summer months, therefore, in the half-hour or so before the evening service or mid-week lunch-hour service, these groups have played, sung and danced on the forecourt outside the church. Some of the dances will be interpretations of a number of worship songs that will be sung during our services; other may be Balkan or Hebrew dances. There is no conscious attempt to 'get across the gospel' in this presentation; but something of our life together in Christ, with the love and joy that we experience in him, is unquestionably communicated, albeit in non-verbal form. Usually a sizeable crowd gathers in no time at all. It senses at once the harmony and happiness of these groups, and (this is the important and significant point) many questions are asked. Why are they so happy? What is it all about? Is it really anything to do with 'church'? Once the questions are being asked, it is most natural for other members of the congregation, mingling with the crowds, to explain something of what we have found in Christ and then to extend an invitation to the service which is about to begin. In this way, many have come, some have met with the living Christ for the first time in their lives, and a few have found him before they left. In themselves, the singing and dancing could be dismissed as being superficial, but they spring from deep relationships that have been formed in Christ, backed by much prayer and a sense of total dependence upon God, and there is no doubt that God has used this simple presentation to communicate powerfully to many people from many different nationalities. Of course a clear explanation of the gospel must follow, if the opportunity is there. But in this apathetic generation, when very few are asking questions, this has proved an astonishingly effective way of getting through to the man in the street — at least initially.

Street theatre, too, can be very effective, and another church I know made a considerable impact by taking singing and drama groups, together with a sizeable section of the congregation, round the streets of the parish. Their corporate witness in this fresh and joyful way drew out a much more positive response than the more traditional door-to-door visiting. Personal contacts were made and later followed up, but the initial interest was undoubtedly sparked off by a glimpse of the living Christ in his body — there on the streets of the parish. It is the communication of *life,* whether or not it is immediately understood as the life of Christ, that makes the impact. Thus it is not the professional quality of the presentation that is the most important factor (although we should aim at the highest standards possible in our given situation), it is rather the living Christ, lived out in the lives and relationships of his people, and expressed in ways that are relevant to the social and cultural setting of that local church.

Here we must trust to the guidance of the Spirit of God. What is right for one church may well not be right for another. It is while the leaders of the church at Antioch were worshipping and praying that the Spirit of God gave them directions for their next move. A firm faith in the sovereignty and creativity of the Spirit should make us hesitant about imitating something that has worked elsewhere, and at the same time make us wide open to fresh and new presentations of the risen Christ, even if they are quite different from anything that we may have previously experienced.

3. NEW SERVICES

New liturgies and experimental services are today common-place within various denominations. Much of this hard work is designed to make the services more intelligible and meaningful for the regular worshipper. So far so good; although we need to remember the point made earlier in this book that, as far as the outsider is concerned, nothing is more meaningful than when he discovers in that church 'a loving, caring community and one which is obviously in love with God and offering real worship. It is reality, not re-arrangement, that will win the pagan and the agnostic.'

Nevertheless, certain forms of service have unquestionably proved their usefulness over the years in the context of evangelism.

GUEST SERVICES

A simple evangelistic service, to which members of a congregation are encouraged to bring their friends, has often been an effective way of leading some people to Christ. Over a period of nine years in York, up to the time of writing this, we have held fifty services of this nature, with many hundreds committing their lives to Christ, coming into an assurance of faith, or discovering some form of spiritual renewal. A theme with a suitable title is first of all chosen, with the aim of finding a subject which is relevant for today and which can lead into a major theme of the gospel. A small committee will then work on the presentation of that chosen theme, so that the whole service unfolds the relevant message of Christ. Christians worshipping together can be a powerful factor in effective evangelism, providing that worship has a note of reality about it with joy inspired by the Holy Spirit. There is a need to be sensitive to those who would find certain patterns of worship quite meaningless. Any prayers, for example, need to be brief, to the point, and at all costs avoiding 'the language of Zion' or other religious jargon which is meaningful (perhaps) only to the initiated. Use is made of drama, dance and mime, either as an expression of worship or an interpretation of a scripture passage, and there could be a place for a personal testimony or an interview. In such a setting, the sermon should aim to spell out some of the truths already proclaimed in a variety of ways, and it should encourage people to face up to the challenge of personal commitment to Christ. It is often helpful to follow the main sermon with a short five-minute summary (perhaps after a quiet song or hymn), which seeks to explain in personal and simple terms what a relationship with Christ really means and how it is possible to start. A closing personal prayer to this effect would be appropriate. Immediately after the service an opportunity should be given for counselling, with an invitation to those who have just prayed that personal prayer to take some literature and any further help that may be necessary. In a local church setting, it is wise to make this invitation in a gentle and sensitive way, understanding the many fears and inhibitions which people have when it comes to any open declaration of a personal faith. At the same time, encouraging people to take a simple step (such as coming up for a booklet) can be a valuable and important way of sealing a new commitment to Christ. Our faith is to be personal but not private, and the Bible undoubtedly links closely together the secret belief in the heart, with the open confession of that faith.[9] Many who are unwilling to do this find that their faith, if genuine at all, goes at once into cold storage, and only begins to become a warm and living faith when such an open confession is made.

The whole question of follow-up is also of the utmost importance. The beginning of a new relationship with Christ is only a beginning, and everyone needs considerable help after that initial step has been taken. Often, at the guest service itself, it is not necessary to do very much in the way of counselling, unless special problems arise; all that is really needed there and then are such details as name and address, approximate age and church link (if any). Wise and mature Christians should, as soon as possible, later in the week, make personal contact so that friendship, practical help and simple instruction in the basics of the faith can be given. A letter, too, from the preacher, arriving a day or two after the service and containing some literature and Bible-reading notes, can be encouraging.

The effectiveness of such a service naturally depends on a number of other factors which lie behind any corporate presentation of the gospel. In the first place, love and harmony within the church itself is vital, and therefore relationship problems must be sorted out. Preparing for a special service must include the healing of any splits, divisions or tensions, or else we shall look for the power of God in vain. It is only as we love one another that God will abide in us and reveal himself to others. This principle is of particular importance for those who may be playing a significant part in the service — ministers; singing, dancing and drama groups; choir, etc. — but it is also relevant for the whole congregation.

In the second place, the priority of prayer cannot be overstressed. When possible, a special time for prayer should be set aside before a guest service, with specific and detailed intercession, covering every aspect of the service and praying for the guests who are expected to come. In all evangelistic work the battle is a demanding and spiritual one, as 'we are not contending against flesh and blood, but against the principalities, against the powers, against the world rulers of this present darkness, against the spiritual hosts of wickedness in the heavenly places'.[10] Failure to take this battle seriously and to claim our authority in Christ over the powers of darkness will almost certainly mean failure in evangelism. We are not playing with words, nor can we hope to persuade men and women out of Satan's Kingdom into God's Kingdom purely by contemporary methods of presentation. In the third place, since worship and praise are themselves powerful, the songs and hymns do not need to be slanted at the outsider. An unbeliever, of course, will not be able to share the deep convictions that are commonly expressed in songs of worship, but if Christians are taken up with loving God and worshipping God, the reality of his presence will be communicated very effectively. Indeed without a sense of his presence our gospel words will seem empty and unreal.

FAMILY SERVICES

These, too, have proved increasingly popular in recent years, and have an unmistakable role in the evangelistic work of a local church. In a largely non-churchgoing population the place of the traditional Sunday School needs to be re-examined. Even large and apparently thriving Sunday Schools speak of an alarming fall-out after the age of eleven or twelve, with comparatively few going on into the full life of the church, and extremely few parents actually being won for Christ. Further, however good the teaching may be for the children on Sundays, the primary and formative influence will undoubtedly come from the home. The family service, however, works on the principle of 'reaching the children through the parents', rather than 'reaching the parents through the children', which has always been one of the principles behind the modern Sunday School. Although the usefulness of the family service may vary from area to area, there is no question that a good many parents are concerned that their children should have a godly and moral foundation laid for their lives, even if they themselves have little or no personal Christian faith. Moreover, since the family as an institution is under attack from various quarters, there is, amongst quite a wide cross-section of society, still some desire to come *en famille* to church, providing the service is short, simple and attractive, with something for the whole family, at least from four or five upwards. In this way, many parents come to church for the sake of their children, when they would not think of coming had they sent their children to Sunday School. Therefore this service becomes one effective way of winning whole families for Christ.

Simple visual aids, the use of projection equipment, soundstrips, drama, puppetry, choruses, criss-cross quizzes, families leading in prayer, perhaps a children's orchestra, maximum participation with children reading the lessons and taking up the offering — these and other ingredients can all help to make up an attractive service. The charge is sometimes made that family services produce a childish spirituality: the milky diet of nursery Christianity which cotton-wools even adults from true discipleship and maturity in Christ. There is little 'solid food' that is offered, and this results in stunted growth. Certainly these dangers are real, but even a weekly family service can play an invaluable role if it is a genuine expression of the life of the family of God in that area, and if it leads on to adult worship and instruction, to Bible-study groups, and to increasing Christian witness and service. Every healthy family should enjoy regular 'family times' together, with everyone involved, including the youngest child. Of course there is a need for more serious and stimulating conversation amongst the adults in the house-hold, but these more relaxed times should be an integral part in the life of a family. So it is in the church. Further, providing the style of teaching is kept simple, and the illustrations and visual aids are such as can appeal to children, it is possible, in the context of this service, to expound almost any spiritual truth. The genius of Christ's teaching was on similar lines: often using natural and visual materials together with magnificent short stories (parables), he proclaimed the most profound principles of the Kingdom of God with superb simplicity. It was the children and ordinary folk who flocked around him so readily: he spoke their language in terms that made sense, even though the most erudite theologians in the world have been grappling with the depths of his teaching ever since.[11]

4. NEW OPPORTUNITIES

HOMES

If a church building is foreign and forbidding territory for most people today, concentrating exclusively on church services would mean ignoring the majority when it comes to evangelism. The home, therefore, becomes a most strategic place when it comes to sharing the good news of Christ. Certainly this was the pattern of the early Church. No doubt the political scene and the persecution, or constant threat of it, made any other platform for the gospel virtually impossible; but, as Michael Green has commented, 'The church in the first three centuries grew without the aid of two of our most prized tools: mass evangelism and evangelism in church. Instead, they used the home.'[12] Certainly the home can be a relaxed setting for the gospel. It imposes no style of worship that is alien to the unbeliever. Misunderstandings and difficulties can be thrashed out. Anyone can take part. Spontaneous testimonies from ordinary church members can be mingled with a simple explanation of the gospel.

As part of a church's long-term evangelistic work, home groups need to be established. One of the really healthy signs in the Church as a whole is the increasing number of fellowship groups meeting in homes, and obviously the precise structuring of these groups will vary. However, the scheme as developed in one church may serve as a practical guide.[13] Where possible the members of each group should be drawn from the immediate area, partly to make it easier in building up relationships during the week and so developing a genuine sense of a caring community. Where there are a number of groups attached to one church, the areas of responsibility need to be fairly carefully defined, although a measure of flexibility will always be necessary in order to meet the special needs of certain people. The groups exist to serve several inter-related purposes: to build up strong relationships between the members in terms of sharing, helping, learning, encouraging, exhorting and rebuking (when necessary); to strengthen one another for work in the church; to help each other in witness, evangelism and service within each area; to stimulate Bible study and prayer, and to share from the Scriptures what God has been saying to each member during the day or week; to be sensitive to the needs of other churches in the area; and to develop some missionary link. It is realised that not every Christian in the area who goes to the same church will want to, or be able to, come to the group meetings, and in that case it is still important to build up good and loving relationships, as far as possible. Each group should also work and pray together with a view to holding at least one or two evangelistic house-meetings each year. The number in the group should not be less than eight, and it is valuable to have at least two homes available for the meetings. The size should not be allowed to grow too large — twelve is about the ideal, with twenty as the absolute maximum, and new groups can be formed either by *division* (one group splitting into two) or by *budding* (two groups re-forming into three). Each group will have its own leader or leaders, although the pastoral care within the group should be the responsibility of all the members, so that the burden of the work does not fall simply on the leader. Nevertheless, the leader must exercise pastoral oversight of the group, be responsible to the minister or elder over him in the church, and be willing to come to regular group leaders' meetings. If he is unable to attend, he must send someone else in his place. These meetings are essential, partly as a training-ground for the leaders, and partly to develop a strong unity amongst the leaders. Indeed, the unity of any church will depend in large measure on the unity amongst the leadership within that church. A wise minister will spend time with the leadership, for this will be the key for the growth and expansion of the whole church.[14]

A special evangelistic house-meeting must, of course, be the united concern of the whole group, and this might well be the first taste of evangelism for some of the members.[15] Each person should be encouraged to think of those whom he can invite, and then to pray for them regularly before the meeting takes place. Personal invitations should be given out two or three weeks before the meeting, and there should be some indication as to the purpose of the meeting. The title of the talk, for example, can be written on the invitation card, and it is wise to use a general and low-key title, such as 'God in Experience', or 'Faith in Focus'. A more direct title, like 'You need Christ!', will be far too threatening for most outsiders. Choose a speaker with a gift for communication in this setting: it must not be a sermon, nor must the talk be long. Usually ten minutes is quite adequate; the purpose is to spark off a valuable discussion on the heart of the Christian faith. Aim to have a cup of tea or coffee when everyone is arriving, and plan for a second one to be available at a strategic moment in order to break up the general discussion into smaller groups.

The smooth running of such an evening may often depend on a number of surprisingly small details. In preparation of a meeting that is not in your home, discuss fully the arrangements with the host and hostess so that they are not nervously uncertain of what to expect; and pray with them. Be there in good time, and see that the chairs are well placed, allowing for maximum communication and good control of the discussion. Have some books and booklets available and well positioned. Keep the meeting itself informal and relaxed throughout, so as to encourage free discussion. Watch out for the red herrings (What about suffering? What about those who have never heard? What about predestination? Was God an astronaut?), and learn to deal quickly with the standard objections to the Christian faith that are raised time and again. Beware of dominating the conversation; aim to draw in other Christians, and encourage spontaneous testimonies. These will often speak more powerfully than a carefully argued case for Christ by someone who is obviously a 'professional'. Allow plenty of time for personal evangelism when the main meeting has broken up, for this will often be the most fruitful part of the whole evening. Be open to the Spirit's leading at this point: some may be ready for prayer there and then; others will benefit from a visit within the next few days. But be sensitive to people as people. Never force yourself or the gospel on someone who is not yet ready. Remember that evangelism is from first to last the sovereign work of the Spirit of God; at best we are to co-operate with him as 'workers together with Christ'.

It is often of special value when a team of Christians from one church visits another church, lives (in pairs if possible) in the homes of the people there, eats with them, prays with them, runs house-meetings with them, and altogether shares Christ with them — if possible for at least one week, maybe two. If this team is backed by prayer from its home church, the blessing all round can be immense. This style of evangelistic mission, moreover, has the considerable added advantage of being comparatively easy to organise, inexpensive to run, natural in style, effective in reaching outsiders, and excellent for the training of ordinary Christians in evangelism. The one or two with the more specialist gifts of evangelistic preaching will be called upon for the Sunday services, which should be looked upon as a time of reaping.

VISITING

In recent years there have been a number of programmes developed and written about, the best-known being Evangelism-in-Depth in Latin America,[16] and Evangelism Explosion in Florida.[17] The details of these schemes can be found elsewhere, but they have the advantage of seeking to mobilise the whole church in its evangelistic work and to draw out in some the gifts for evangelism that they might not have known were there. However, in general terms, although there may be some value in knocking on every door in a given area at regular intervals, the most fruitful visiting will usually be selective. It will often be best to spend time in following up contacts that have already been made as a result of baptisms, weddings, funerals, and occasional visits to church services. Often these contacts will give some indication as to where the Spirit of God is already at work, and time given to these homes will almost certainly be worth far more than hours and hours of 'peddling faith to the sceptical'. Of course the patient and more demanding door-to-door work may bring to light a number of people who are hungry for God and who would not be contacted in any other way, and therefore this system is not to be despised nor dismissed. But in my experience it is seldom fruitful, and each church must constantly work out its priorities in terms of evangelism. From the gospel records it is apparent that Jesus frequently concentrated on one needy individual, or on twelve disciples. This, to him, was often more valuable than scattering his energies superficially amongst the crowds.

LITERATURE

The most effective political and religious movements have always known the power of the printed page. What men think is largely determined by what they read. The influence of the media on the lives of people today is incalculable. For this reason Bishop John Taylor has written:

> There are days when I hate the printed word. The printed word is manipulated to convince people of what is not true, to arouse unnecessary fears, appetites and angers, to divert attention from things that ought to be called in question, and to encourage a trivial approach to all the important issues... The only antidote to lies is to publish the truth — true facts, true interpretations, true values, true emotions, true objectives.

Much of the material that people see on television, hear from the radio or read in the dailies, is utterly different from the truths and standards of God's word. There is therefore an urgent need to use attractive and relevant literature to feed the minds of countless millions of people throughout the world who are experiencing 'a famine...of hearing the words of the Lord'.[18] In the mission of the Church, money that is spent on evangelistic books, booklets, leaflets, magazines and newspapers is money well spent — providing that the format of this literature makes for good communication.

CASSETTES

Imaginative uses of tapes and cassettes, and of local radio, can all form a further arm in the outreach of the church. In York we started a tape library from the smallest beginnings; it was almost by accident that we started at all. Within three or four years well over 1,000 cassettes were sent out each year, many of them directly or indirectly related to evangelism. I know of other churches which send out 20,000 tapes a year, or more. This can be a simple yet remarkably powerful means of communicating the gospel to home groups or to individuals who might otherwise hear very little of the love and truth of Jesus Christ.

5. NEW LIVES

The youth work of any church is of crucial importance both for the present and for the future. A church that neglects the young is a dying church. But if a church is to be relevant for young people, it must keep on its toes. It must change, in some measure at least, as the culture changes; it must be fresh and flexible in its presentation of the gospel; it must allow room for young blood to come into positions of responsibility, leadership and ministry; it must rejoice when young people not only take over some of the positions held by older members but also do the jobs more effectively; it must release its finest leaders to give maximum time and attention to the young; it must be understanding when faced with immature zeal, misguided energy, or damage to church property; it must, at all costs, 'hold unfailing love' towards young people so that they know they are really wanted within God's family. A church that is unwilling to do this is digging its own grave. Further, the ministers and leaders of a church must learn to listen. What are the questions being asked by the young today? What problems do they find with the Church? What do they feel is irrelevant? What are the issues in society and in the world that really concern them? What are the personal cries and frustrations in their own hearts? What are the temptations and pressures that they face? What communicates to them? How can the message of Christ get through to them in ways that make sense? And who, within the family of the Church, have been given by God the gifts to relate to them at some depth? Such members ought to receive every possible encouragement to give themselves wholeheartedly to the task of building tomorrow's Church. I know of several clergy or ministers who would rather employ a full-time youth leader, who could concentrate on this one job, than a curate or assistant minister who would very likely be involved with a variety of other responsibilities as well.

6. CHURCH GROWTH

The magazine *Decision* over a period of several years conducted a survey on seventeen local churches (in North America, Australia and England) which had seen remarkable growth. They discovered certain characteristics that were common to all the churches:

Prayer. All the churches studied placed so much emphasis on prayer that it could be said that nothing of importance took place in the church life without prayer. Half-nights of prayer, prayer breakfasts, staff prayers, prayer retreats, daily regular and special prayer sessions, healing services, laying-on-of-hands, were all part of the pattern, depending on the church.

Witnessing. A good proportion of the congregation was actively engaged in sharing a personal knowledge of Jesus Christ with others. This was done by individual activity, through small groups, visitation and penetration teams, or in the body life of the church.

Conversions. People were actually being saved in these churches, weekly and even daily (Acts 2:47). In many of them a holy expectation was present whenever the congregation gathered. People wondered, 'Who will be next?' Teams of laymen and young people were leading others to Christ, not just in the neighbourhood but as far away as Hawaii, Korea and Japan.

Joy. The people liked to walk through the church doors; it was a good place to be. But it was more than a clubby atmosphere; people were talking about the Lord, telling about answers to prayer, praising God.

Scripture. The entire educational programme of the church was built around the Bible. Not only did the pastors preach from Scripture, the people were learning to use it through discipleship training. The absolute authority of Scripture was accepted in every one of the churches.

Preaching. Messages delivered from the pulpit were well prepared, Bible-based, with good outlines and effective use of illustrations. The preacher did his homework.

Outreach. Each church was investing heavily in national and international mission activities. Some were involved in inner-city work, some in special ministries to the deaf, the retarded, senior citizens, vacationers on the beaches. All were budgeting up to and even beyond 50 per cent for missionary causes.

Family Life. Each of the congregations cultivated a warm church family atmosphere. Even though the membership was growing by leaps and bounds, the pastoral team managed to convey the impression of ministering to a small, intimate family.

Leadership. The 'prima donna' complex was absent from the church's leadership. A gracious reciprocal spirit permeated staff relationships and filtered through to the congregation.

Love. The most important quality common to all the churches was the spirit of love that embraced everyone who walked through the church doors, regardless of background, status, skin-colour or life-style. There were no walls or false faces; people seemed eager to bear each other's burdens. The pastors' love for the people was expressed, accepted and returned.

The Report went on to say that no doubt there were other factors involved in the growth of these churches, but those ten points seemed to be of special significance. 'We believe,' the Report concluded, 'that if any church seeks to pursue them with determination, it will find God blessing its own congregational life with solid, Spirit-filled growth.'

NOTES

1   R. Halverson, quoted in *Is Revolution Change?*
    by Brian Griffiths (I.V.P.) 87f, p. 134.
2   Ephesians 2:12-22, p. 137.
3   Bryan Ellis, from a paper 'Christians in Industrial
    Areas', p. 137.
4   1 Corinthians 14:1; 1 Peter 3:11, p. 138.
5   J. McFadden, 'To Love as Jesus Loved',
    in *New Covenant*, May 1975, 21, p. 139.
6   2 Timothy 1:13f, p. 139.
7   Romans 15:18f, p. 140.
8   Acts 21:11, p. 140.
9   Romans 10:9f, p. 144.
10 Ephesians 6:12, p. 145.
11 For an excellent and comprehensive book on
    family services, see M. Botting, *Teaching the Families*
    (Falcon), p. 145.
12 *Let the Earth Hear His Voice*, 169, p. 147.
13 St Michael-le-Belfrey, York, p. 147.
14 See *Urban Church Project*, Report No. 5, for helpful
    comments. Obtainable from 19 Bosworth Road,
    Dagenham, Essex, p. 148.
15 I am grateful to the Revd. Gavin Reid for some
    of the suggestions regarding this theme, p. 149.
16 See W. D. Roberts; *Revolution in Evangelism*
    (Scripture Union), p. 150.
17 See D. J. Kennedy, *Evangelism Explosion* (Coverdale), p. 150.
18 Amos 8:11, p. 151.

CHAPTER NINE

Worship and Evangelism

IN HIS FIRST letter, Peter writes that those who come to Christ
have a two-fold priority: first to worship and secondly to
witness.

> Come to him, to that living stone, rejected by men but in
> God's sight chosen and precious; and like living stones be
> yourselves built into a spiritual house, to be a holy
> priesthood, to offer spiritual sacrifices acceptable to God
> thorough Jesus Christ... You are a chosen race, a royal
> priesthood, a holy nation, God's own people, that you may
> declare the wonderful deeds of him who called you out of
> darkness into his marvellous light.[1]

Not surprisingly, therefore, there is a close link between
worship and witness, worship and evangelism, worship and
service. Indeed, both the Hebrew and Greek languages use
one main word which could be translated as either worship or
work.[2] Yet the importance of worship in the realm of
evangelism has often been neglected. In the 1,470 page report
of the Lausanne Congress on World Evangelisation, for
example, there are only two short paragraphs specifically on
worship. However, on many occasions I have seen the close
link between the praise of God, when marked by the freshness
and freedom of the Spirit's presence, and powerful evangelism. Quite often during a communion service (Church of
England, Series 3, for example), when both service and
sermon were directed almost exclusively to the convinced

believer, I have seen men and women brought to faith in Christ, largely through the praise of God's people.

What then is worship? It is not always readily understood. At a five-day conference for Christian leaders I became increasingly aware of the fact that, after four heady days of lectures, seminars and Bible studies, we had not as a group ever once really worshipped God in praise. I talked to the leader of the conference about this. He agreed with me about this neglect. It was eventually decided to have a half hour's hymn singing before the next session! My heart sank, and I realised more than ever how vitally important at least a taste of real worship was at that particular conference.

One of the most famous and most comprehensive definitions of worship comes from William Temple:

> Worship is the submission of all our nature to God. It is the quickening of conscience by his holiness; the nourishment of mind with his truth; the purifying of imagination by his beauty; the opening of the heart to his love; the surrender of will to his purpose — and all this gathered up in adoration, the most selfless emotion of which our nature is capable.[3]

It is worth noticing that this same definition could serve very well for evangelism.

The New Testament, in fact, speaks of three main aspects of worship, which are different but closely related. *First, there is worship by our bodies.* Paul, havin expounded on the immeasurable grace of God to sinners, comes to an obvious practical challenge: 'I appeal to you therefore, brethren, by the mercies of God, to present your bodies as a living sacrifice, holy and acceptable to God, which is your spiritual worship.'[4] The phrase 'living sacrifice' must have been especially striking for a Jew who for centuries had been accustomed to the idea of a dead sacrifice: it was the ultimate offering to God, the total surrender of a life, with no reservations. Of course this will not be easy; but as King David once declared, 'I will not offer...to the Lord my God [that]which cost me nothing.'[5] A sacrifice will inevitably be costly, and a 'living sacrifice' implies that it will continue to be costly and painful;

but worship means worth-ship, and we can only bring to him the total response of our lives — nothing less than this is worthy of God who has given us his only Son. Paul, then, goes on in the rest of Romans, Chapter 12, to spell out what the worship of God really involves. It means not being conformed to this world, but being transformed by the constant renewing of our minds according to the will of God. It means using every God-given gift to build up the Body of Christ — prophecy, service, teaching, sharing, helping, or whatever it may be. It means genuine love, generous giving, warm hospitality, harmonious relationships, unceasing forgiveness, and more and more love. Worship is not the occupation of an hour or two once a week in a religious building; it is the devotion of a whole life. Here we have much to learn from the revolutionary groups of today. Worship has been defined as the submission of the whole being to the object of worship, and there are many in the world who are dedicating everything to the Party or the cause. This has always been the principle behind effective revolution.

> Could anyone have predicted that the tiny handful of disciples at Pentecost would eventually conquer the mighty Roman Empire? There were only 120 of them among an estimated four million Jews in Palestine. That's a ratio of 1 to 33,000. It's as if there were only 6,000 believers in the entire US. One per cent of the Russians brought about the Russian Revolution. Nazism was always a minority until it was too late. A leader of the radical student Left recently told Billy Graham that they were trying to cut their movement down by two-thirds until they had a dedicated group of trained and disciplined followers who could bring about the revolution.[6]

Such dedication is one vital aspect of worship.

Secondly, there is worship by our praise. In a solemn passage which speaks about suffering for Christ, discipline by God, obedience to leaders, and bearing abuse for the sake of the Master, the writer to the Hebrews goes on to say, 'Through him then let us continually offer up a sacrifice of praise to God, that is, the fruit of lips that acknowledge his name.'[7]

Clearly in a tough and painful situation there may be little spontaneous and overflowing desire to praise the Lord. That is why we are called to offer him a *sacrifice* of praise. 'Great is the Lord and greatly to be praised,' says the psalmist.[8] We praise him, not because we feel like it, nor necessarily because we have remembered some of the marvellous things that he has done for us, but simply because he is the Lord and therefore always worthy of our praise. We praise him for his majesty and sovereignty, that he is infinite in wisdom and glorious in power, steadfast in his love and unceasing in his mercy. And when we offer him the praise of our lips in order to glorify him, God will always honour that offering. He may come down upon us in fresh love and power, moving freely amongst us by his Spirit. Others may become aware of God's presence, perhaps for the very first time, and are therefore much more open to receive God's word and God's truth. On numerous occasions, after a time of genuine and powerful worship and praise, I have found it much easier proclaiming the good news of Jesus Christ. It is as though I am able to say, 'Here is the truth of what you have already, in some measure, seen and heard'; and it is significant that Peter was able to say precisely that to the crowd at Pentecost. When the disciples were filled with the Holy Spirit and were able to praise God in languages given to them by the Spirit, Peter went on to explain to everyone what it was all about. His sermon was not a matter of empty words or theoretical doctrines; in his preaching of Christ he was able to say, 'Having received from the Father the promise of the Holy Spirit, he has poured out this which you see and hear.'[9] It was in the outpouring of the Holy Spirit, with the consequent heart-felt praise, that God had already manifested himself. How effective it was, then, to preach about what they had already witnessed for themselves, even though the reality of what they had seen and heard still needed to be interpreted. Hector Espinoza has summed it up well in these words:

Worship should function as the means by which the people of God are built up in the Spirit in order to move out into the unredeemed world with an authentic, effective witness to the reality of God and to his great love made known to us in Jesus Christ. In the course of worship, even though it is primarily directed to the needs of the believers and represents the Godward expression of the Lord's people, the unbeliever may well catch sight of God and thus be brought to faith.[10]

The Jews had three main words for praise, and the primary meaning of these words is 'making a noise' (usually with the human voice), 'playing an instrument' and 'moving the body'.[11] Singing has always, of course, been a basic ingredient of praise, and although there should be some theological content in a song before it becomes a valid expression of praise, there is something to be said for what amounts to a sung meditation on the nature or character of God — especially in these days when the emphasis in the world is on speed. Therefore there can be a real place for simple and often repetitive worship choruses, providing this continues to be genuine worship and not vain repetition. After all, in Psalm 136 the words 'For his steadfast love endures for ever' come no less than twenty-six times! And in most of our great Easter hymns we sing the word *Hallelujah!* over and over again. In some circles there has been an unfair and biblically unjustifiable resistance . to simple and repetitive worship choruses, although certainly there are some obvious dangers which need to be watched.

When it comes to 'playing an instrument', virtually any instrument can be brought into the praise of God: Psalm 150 speaks of the trumpet, lute, harp, timbrel, strings, pipe and loud clashing cymbals all uniting in the worship of God. Most congregations will have a variety of people who can play a variety of instruments but who are sitting passively in their pews whilst one man dominates the scene on the organ. How much better it is to use the gifts that God has already given, and to encourage maximum involvement and participation.

Concerning 'moving the body', it may be necessary to look in a little more detail at the whole question of dance in worship. A number of bishops in the fifteenth century tried to stamp out dancing in church on the grounds that it was because of dancing that John the Baptist lost his head! I have not heard that argument put forward in recent days, but still there is considerable suspicion, caution and fear amongst some Christians as the whole practice of dancing is steadily coming back into the context of worship. Certainly dancing was a natural and regular part of worship in Old Testament days, and quite possibly in New Testament days as well. It is always dangerous to argue from silence (there is nothing specifically about dancing in the New Testament), but at least there is nothing whatever to suggest that this practice, which had been an integral part of the religious life of God's people for many centuries, had ceased, and indeed it would be strange if it had to cease, since Christ came to bring fulness of joy and the wine of the Spirit. The early Church, of course, had no church buildings in which to meet, and doubtless the comparatively small homes of believers made dancing difficult. Thus it is not surprising that it is only in the fourth century, when church buildings began to be built, that we have any clear evidence of dancing as an authentic form of Christian worship.

As we turn to the Scriptures we see points worth noting about dancing. First, dancing was sometimes prophetic in its associations. It was no accident, for example, that it was Miriam the prophetess who led the dance after the crossing of the Red Sea. Dance was one way by which God spoke to his people, and that is still true today. When the spirit of prophecy fell upon King Saul, he was caught up in a feverish dance, yet it was no mere ecstasy, but real communication between God and his servant. Dance can often 'say' things in a certain situation beyond the scope of mere words. Secondly, dancing usually involved a group of women (as in Exodus 15:20-1), but not always so. King David, and quite possibly other kings too, danced before the Lord. He was despised by Michal for his enthusiasm in worship, but he replied that what he had done was 'before the Lord...and I will make merry before the Lord'.[12] The main Hebrew word for a pilgrim festival is *hag,* and some commentators suggest that this term arose because of the dance of the pilgrims. Thus, in Psalm 42 for example, the psalmist remembers how once he 'led them in procession [dance?] to the house of God, with glad shouts and songs of thanksgiving, a multitude keeping festival' (the festal procession dance, *hogeg*).

Thirdly, dancing was often the climax in worship. After Moses and the people sang a song to the Lord, Miriam and 'all the women' picked up the same song and brought it to a climax in the dance. Dancing, when it is an interpretation of a song of praise, is like a descant in movement. Fourthly, dancing was one recognised form of proclaiming God's good news, and therefore should be rightly linked with evangelism. In fact, some dancers were actually called 'evangelists'. For example, in Psalm 68:11f. we read, 'The Lord gives the command: great is the host of those who bore the tidings: "The kings of the armies, they flee, they flee!"' Here the Hebrew word for 'those who bore the tidings' is the feminine form of the word 'evangelist'; and a better translation of verse 11 might read, 'The women that proclaim the good news are a great host.' In practice, the good news of God's victory was proclaimed in a great procession led by women, some of whom were prophetesses, who were singing and dancing. This was one God-given way in which the Spirit of God encouraged people with the sense of God's presence and power, and consequently led them out into worship. Here all the faculties of mind and soul and body were united in praise, and this was one authentic way of enjoying and sharing the experience of the living God. 'The call and the impulse to enjoy the manifest God run like electric charges through prophets, priests, psalmists, musicians and dancers to the whole "family of Zion".'[13] Moreover, this is far from being purely an interesting historical detail of Israelite culture. Recently I have on numerous occasions witnessed the same moving of the Spirit of God through united singing and dancing, springing out from the sharing of lives together in Jesus Christ. Not only has this stimulated God's people to worship and praise, but outsiders, with no professed belief at all, have often tasted, perhaps for the first time, something of the joy and presence of the living God.

Worship, then, involves our bodies and our praise. *Thirdly, there is worship by our possessions.* 'Do not neglect to do good and to share what you have, for such sacrifices are pleasing to God.'[14] The New Testament Church was marked by great generosity, and this was one of the clearest signs of God's grace in its life. Paul describes the astonishing giving of the

Christians in Macedonia: 'In a severe test of affliction, their abundance of joy and their extreme poverty have overflowed in a wealth of liberality on their part. For they gave according to their means, as I can testify, and beyond their means, of their own free will.'[15] Paul uses this example to stir up the Corinthian Church 'to excel in this gracious work also'. For, as he goes on to remark, 'the rendering of this service [*leitourgia,* from which comes our English word 'liturgy'] not only supplies the wants of the saints but also overflows in many thanksgivings to God. Under the test of this service, you will glorify God by your obedience in acknowledging the gospel of Christ'.[16] A strong critic of the Church once explained what confirmed his position as an unbeliever: 'The Church has never learnt the secret of community.' And yet this was undoubtedly a major part of the immense appeal of the New Testament Church. They were of one heart and soul, and instead of clinging to their own personal possessions they had everything in common so that 'there was not a needy person among them'. Their loving fellowship in Christ was the clearest demonstration of the truth of the gospel. This is why Christ stressed that mutual love was the new commandment he had given to his disciples, and it was to be their distinguishing mark. A radiant love for Christ and for fellow-Christians is the surest mark of the Spirit's presence, for love is of God. Nothing is more powerful in witness than a fellowship of believers who have become, no doubt through pain and suffering, trial and temptation, an authentic community of love.

One obvious expression of this is the extended family. It is not the only expression of a caring community, nor the best pattern for everyone, but it is a good and valid way of living as Christians and one that is growing in some churches.

Most famous, perhaps, has been the development in the Church of the Holy Redeemer in Houston, Texas,[17] but other churches and communities have also experienced the considerable value — and some of the dangers — of this particular form of life-style. Usually a number of persons, single or divorced or widowed, come to share their lives with a nuclear family; or perhaps a number of single people live together; or perhaps two or more families join forces. In this way it is possible to live much more simply and cheaply (some households will develop the principle of a common purse), and this factor releases both money and manpower for the work of the Kingdom of God. Some members of a household will be breadwinners, releasing others for full-time work in the Church. It is an excellent way for learning basic lessons concerning the Body of Christ, such as commitment to one another and the spirit of service; it provides support both for those engaged in a demanding ministry and for those with special needs; it has great healing potential and it can help to strengthen individuals for service in the Church; it can speak powerfully of the love and reality of Christ to the world. However, whether the growth of community involves Christians coming together under one roof or not, sharing what we have with one another is a sacrifice 'pleasing to God', and therefore one ingredient of worship.

True worship, which can play such an important part in effective communication and evangelism, is thus a fully-orbed affair. Great singing, if divorced from the surrender of our lives and the sharing of our possessions, can be superficial and deceptive; it will be unlikely to communicate anything of the reality of Christ. And sacrificial service and generous giving require the warmth of genuine praise before anything of the love of Christ is mediated. All three aspects of worship are important. Moreover, it is interesting to note how often in the Bible worship is directly associated with a demonstration of God's power. For example, in the building of the Temple, King David led God's people in some extremely sacrificial giving, both of their possessions and of their lives: 'with a whole heart they offered freely to the Lord.'[18] Therefore, with this as the basis of their worship, it is not surprising that at the dedication of the Temple the sacrifice of praise released the power and glory of the Lord. 'When the song was raised, with trumpets and cymbals and other musical instruments, in praise to the Lord...the house of the Lord was filled with a cloud, so that the priests could not stand to minister because of the cloud; for the glory of the Lord filled the house of God.'[19] Or again, when the children of Israel, under the leadership of Jehoshaphat, were faced with an overwhelmingly powerful army coming against them, there was no question of the dedication of their lives to God; they were willing to lay down their lives for his sake. However, they fell down before the Lord, worshipping the Lord; and they sent singers on ahead of the army to continue to praise the Lord as a sign of their confidence in him and of their faith in the promise he had given concerning his victory. 'And when they began to sing and praise', the Lord routed the enemy in a remarkable display of his power.[20]

Turning to the New Testament, we notice the same impact of praise with the evangelistic work of the Church. We have already noted the obvious example in Acts, Chapter 2, on the day of Pentecost. Then in Acts, Chapter 4, when Peter and John were warned by the same rulers who had murdered Jesus not to teach any more in his name, they joined the rest of the disciples for a time of prayer. The burden of their prayer was the theme of confident trust in the sovereign Lord. They praised him that he was the God of creation, the God of revelation, and the God of history. They praised him that even the powerful enemies of Jesus could do only what his hand and his plan had predestined to take place. But they did not leave it with this time of praise. Nor did they ask for safety, nor for God's direct and spectacular intervention in the perilous situation in which they found themselves. Instead they asked God to help them to speak his word with all boldness, trusting him to stretch out his hand to heal and to confirm their word with signs and wonders. They were then filled with the Holy Spirit and spoke the word of God with boldness. Moreover, within their loving fellowship they shared their money and possessions; they had everything in common. In other words, here was a wonderful illustration of worship by their praise, by their lives and by their possessions; and it is not surprising, in that context, that 'with great power the apostles gave their testimony to the resurrection of the Lord Jesus'.

In Acts, Chapter 13, we find a similar situation. It was while the teachers and prophets of the church at Antioch were worshipping the Lord and fasting that the Holy Spirit gave them instructions about their next missionary move. As part of the living sacrifice of their lives they instantly obeyed, and after further fasting and prayer sent off Barnabas and

Saul for the work to which God had called them — a sacrifice, incidentally, not only for Barnabas and Saul, but also for the church at Antioch who were willing to release such key leaders in their fellowship. No wonder God continued to honour such worship, and that at one place 'the whole city gathered together to hear the word of God' — the impact that they made for Christ was tremendous. Or again, in Acts, Chapter 16, we find Paul and Silas praying and singing hymns to God in prison and at midnight. This must have been a considerable sacrifice of praise, as they had just been afflicted with many blows and their feet were fastened in the stocks. Yet God honoured their praise, and when a 'great earthquake' threw the whole place into confusion, it is understandable that the jailer, filled with fear, sought out Paul and Silas and asked them, 'What must I do to be saved?' It is not stretching the point too far to say that this evangelistic opportunity came partly as a result of praise.

Clearly it would be wrong to *use* worship as a *tool* for evangelism. True worship must always be first and foremost God-ward in its direction, even though the expression of worship, certainly in terms of serving and giving, may bring much blessing to other people. But when we are taken up with worship, and when we are unashamed of the fact that we are in love with God and in love with one another, that can be very powerful indeed. The world today is starved of love, suffocated with words, bereft of joy, and lacking in peace. Therefore 'a praising community preaches to answer questions raised by its praise'. So often, today, evangelism is crippled by the prevailing apathy. Comparatively few people are asking serious questions about God, partly because there is little or nothing which they see or hear to awake them to any sense of his reality. But when Christians are to be found really worshipping God, loving him, serving him, excited with him, and when their worship makes them into a caring community of love, then questions will certainly be asked, leading to excellent opportunities for sharing the good news of Christ.

NOTES

1   1 Peter 2:4-5, 9, p. 156.
2   *abad, latreuo*, p. 156.
3   *Readings in St. John's Gospel* (Macmillan), 68, p. 157.
4   Romans 12:1, p. 157.
5   2 Samuel 24:24, p. 157.
6   L. Ford, *One Way to Change the World* (Coverdale), 90, p. 158.
7   Hebrews 13:15, p. 158.
8   Psalm 48:1, p. 159.
9   Acts 2:33, p. 159.
10 *Let the Earth Hear His Voice*, 1101, p. 159.
11 *halal, zamar, yada*, p. 160.
12 2 Samuel 6:16-23, p. 161.
13 From J. H. Eaton, essay in *Worship and Dance*,
    ed. J. G. Davies, a symposium from the
    University of Birmingham, p. 162.
14 Hebrews 13:16, p. 162.
15 2 Corinthians 8:2f, p. 163.
16 2 Corinthians 9:12f, p. 163.
17 Well described in M. Harper, *A New Way of
    Living* (Hodder & Stoughton). See also
    Dave and Neta Jackson, *Living Together
    in a World Falling Apart* (Creation House), p. 163.
18 1 Chronicles 29, p. 164.
19 2 Chronicles 5:13f, p. 164.
20 2 Chronicles 20, p. 165.

CHAPTER TEN

The Spirit in Evangelism

THE ACTS OF the Apostles records an astonishing growth-rate of the first-century Christian Church. How could such a very ordinary and somewhat nervous band of 120 disciples, huddled together in prayer in that upper room, launch such a devastating spiritual revolution that the fiercest persecution could not stamp it out? Instead, not only were huge numbers led to faith in Jesus Christ, but also inroads were made into the mighty Roman Empire with increasing power until the Emperor himself was converted two centuries later.

What were the reasons for this extraordinary evangelism explosion? Why has the Church at certain other times and in other places seen at least a similar thrust with the gospel of Christ? And what is missing when the ineffectiveness and irrelevance of the Church is all too apparent?

In the first generation of the Church we must not forget the uniqueness of the apostolic witness and the clearly exceptional effusion of God's grace for the period when the foundation of the entire Christian Church was being laid. Paul wrote that the household of God was 'built upon the foundation of the apostles and prophets, Christ Jesus himself being the chief cornerstone'.[1] Therefore, when 'many wonders and signs were done among the people by the hands of the apostles', so that the sick were brought out into the street in the hope that at least Peter's shadow might fall on some of them,[2] and when 'God did extraordinary miracles [even Luke recognised that these were not 'ordinary' miracles!] by the hands of Paul, so that handkerchiefs or aprons were carried away from his body to the sick, and diseases left them and the evil spirits came out of them[3], it is not to be assumed that the same astonishing power is available to all Christians in every generation. Of course God in his sovereignty *may* give quite remarkable signs and wonders at any time, and the history of the Christian Church up to the present day contains numerous evidences (persuasive to all but the determinedly sceptical) that healings and miracles and other less common gifts of the Holy Spirit did not die out with the apostles. However, there was no doubt a special and unusual cluster of miracles surrounding the apostolic testimony to the resurrection of the Lord Jesus.

Having said all that, the manifest power of God that was demonstrated so fruitfully in the New Testament Church was, of course, the power of the Holy Spirit. There are no less than forty specific references to the Spirit in the first thirteen chapters of Acts. If Luke's second volume bears the right title, as it is largely an account of the various activities of the apostles, a fuller and more accurate title would be 'The Acts of the Apostles through the power of the Holy Spirit'. Let us look, then, at a number of aspects of the Spirit's work in relation to evangelism.

1. *The Holy Spirit and the Great Commission.* The Spirit of God is essentially a witnessing Spirit. 'He will bear witness to me, and you also are witnesses,' said Jesus.[4] 'I will send him to you. And when he comes [to you], he will convince the world of sin and of righteousness and of judgment.'[5] This is the great purpose of God's gift of his Spirit to us: to make us more effective in our witness and evangelism. 'You shall receive power when the Holy Spirit has come upon you; and you shall be my witnesses.'[6] Indeed, whenever and wherever the Spirit is present in power, the evangelistic work of the Church will flow naturally and spontaneously.

The urge to witness is inborn in the Church, it is given with her nature, with her very being. She cannot not-witness. She has this being because of the Spirit who indwells her. Pentecost made the Church a witnessing Church because at Pentecost the witnessing Spirit identified himself with the Church and made the Great

Commission the law of her life... [From that time on] the obedience of the Church to the law of her being was a natural obedience, unreflective, spontaneous. It was the response of a healthy organism to the law of its life. 'We cannot but speak the things that we have seen and heard.' Acts 4:20. So spontaneous was the response of the Church to the Spirit-effected law...that the need of consciously obeying the command of Christ was not felt... It formed no part of her motivation.[7]

From this it could be said that having to stress the Great Commission, and having to urge people to witness, is not a sign of spiritual life, but a sign of spiritual decadence.

Certainly from Pentecost onwards, evangelism inevitably happened. It was not long before the accusation came to the Church leaders from the high priest: 'You have filled Jerusalem with your teaching.'[8] And yet we find no reference at all in the early Church to that Great Commission. Nowhere does Luke suggest that they reminded one another or exhorted one another to 'go and preach the gospel'. Even in Acts, Chapters 11 and 15, where Luke records the momentous debate concerning the gospel for the Gentiles, there is no appeal to Christ's Commission, but only to the fact that the Holy Spirit was so obviously at work amongst the Gentiles that the Church ought to acknowledge what God was clearly doing. The encouragements to evangelise were unnecessary when the witnessing Spirit was so powerfully working amongst them. The irresistible missionary expansion of the Church was inevitable from the precise moment that the Spirit descended upon those disciples in that upper room. In the various calls to mission from Church leaders today, the seeming ineffectiveness of much of the subsequent evangelism may well be due to a failure to appropriate the power of the Spirit. Only the Holy Spirit can bestow spiritual life, and if there is no life there will be no powerful preaching of the gospel, and where there is no powerful preaching of the gospel there will be no transmission of life to others. The only way out of this impasse is to look for, ask for, and receive the power of the Spirit. No exhortations to evangelise, no calls to mission, no reminders of the Great Commission can ever be a substitute for the revitalising, energising work of the witnessing Spirit.

2. *The Holy Spirit and Power.* Shortly before his ascension, Jesus said to his disciples:

> 'Thus it is written, that the Christ should suffer and on the third day rise from the dead, and that repentance and forgiveness of sins should be preached in his name to all nations, beginning from Jerusalem. You are witnesses of these things. And behold, I send the promise of my Father upon you; but stay in the city, until you are clothed with power from on high.'[9]

It is useless to attempt to witness to Christ, in obedience to his command, without the power of his Spirit. It is out of the abundance of the heart that the mouth will speak. For example, if you are carrying a glass full of some liquid and if I bump into you, what will spill out? Naturally, whatever is in that glass. In the same way, when people 'bump into' us each day in the street, shop, office, lecture room or hospital, what will spill out of our hearts? Obviously whatever is in them. That is why the disciples were told to wait until their hearts were filled with the Spirit; without this they would have been empty and powerless to communicate Christ. Nor was the coming of the Spirit at Pentecost sufficient for them on all subsequent occasions. Shortly afterwards, feeling their weakness under the threat of persecution, they prayed to God for boldness, 'and they were all filled with the Holy Spirit and spoke the word of God with boldness... And with great power the apostles gave their testimony to the resurrection of the Lord Jesus.'[10] Indeed the power of the Spirit is indispensable to the proclamation of the gospel. Anyone can preach words; some can preach convincing and persuasive words; but only God can change lives. Paul knew the absolute importance of this. Coming to the sin-city of Corinth he later wrote, 'I was with you in weakness and in much fear and trembling; and my speech and my message were not in plausible words of wisdom, but in demonstration of the Spirit and power, that your faith might not rest in the wisdom of men but in the power of God.'[11] And to the Thessalonians he wrote that 'our gospel came to you not only in word, but also in power and in the Holy Spirit and with full conviction' *(plerophoria)*.[12] This word *plerophoria* is an interesting word. In contrast to the ceaseless chatter and empty sophistry of the pagan world, Paul's message was not only relevant and true, but it was also convincingly full of the Spirit of God. It carried the authority and power of God himself. In this the apostles were true ambassadors of Christ, for he frequently astonished his hearers by the authority with which he spoke.

Luke several times links the power of the Spirit with obedience to God. Although the heavenly Father gives the Spirit to those who ask him,[13] the power of this gift will be released only when we obey him. When Jesus went into his wilderness temptations he was *full* of the Spirit, but having, in obedience to his Father, resisted those six weeks of severe testing, he 'returned in the *power* of the Spirit' and went straight into his astounding ministry.[14] Then when the apostles were brought before the very council responsible for the death of their Master and were charged not to teach in his name, Peter boldly replied, 'We must obey God rather than men.' Then after a brief summary of the gospel, he went on to say, 'And we are witnesses to these things, and so is the Holy Spirit whom God has given to those who obey him' — meaning, in the context, obeying God by continuing to witness to Jesus no matter what anyone says! Well, of course the members of the council were enraged by this, and they beat the apostles and charged them again not to speak in the name of Jesus. But the apostles 'left the presence of the council, rejoicing that they were counted worthy to suffer dishonour for the name. And every day in the temple and at home they did not cease teaching and preaching Jesus as the Christ.'[15] No wonder the power of God was with them! And no wonder we read shortly afterwards that 'the word of God increased; and the number of the disciples multiplied greatly in Jerusalem, and a great many of the priests were obedient to the faith'.[16] Stephen, too, was 'full of grace and power' because he was willing to be obedient literally unto death. His supreme desire was to glorify Christ, whether by life or by death. No wonder his face was like the face of an angel! Of course the power of God was mightily with him. Although he was originally chosen as one of the seven to look after the practical needs of widows, God so honoured his commitment to Christ that he 'did great wonders and signs among the people'.[17]

In all these instances the power of the Spirit was manifestly present because these men were totally committed to Christ and also to one another, regardless of the personal consequences. This, by and large, is what is lacking in the Church today, and consequently there is so little power, or even motivation, when it comes to evangelism. Taking the Church as a whole, we are not single-minded when it comes to our commitment to Christ or to the Body of Christ. Either we have many interests and ambitions, the Kingdom of God being only one of them, in which case the Church becomes simply one of many clubs to which we belong, and our involvement is determined by our inclination at that time, or we are committed to Christ in a personal and private fashion, but not to the Body of Christ. We remain individualists, and avoid one of the immediate implications of being filled with the Spirit, namely 'submitting to one another out of reverence for Christ'.[18] However, God's power is for God's people. It was when the disciples 'lifted their voices *together* to God' and 'were of *one* heart and soul', and 'had everything in *common*' that 'great grace was upon them *all*'.[19]

3. *The Holy Spirit and Communication.* The Spirit is concerned not primarily with religious experiences, but with the truth of the gospel of Christ and with the truth of God's word. Jesus called him the Spirit of truth who would guide the disciples into all the truth.[20] Now the truth without the Spirit can be depressing and damaging in its deadness; but the Spirit — or rather spiritual experiences — without the truth can quickly slide into all kinds of excesses, abuses and counterfeits. 'The Spirit is bound to the word... A Church which abandons the link with the word and tries to rely only on the Spirit falls a prey to all the evils of spiritualistic enthusiasm. Conversely, a Church which tries to rely only on the word and tries to reduce the Spirit to the word, falls a prey to all the evils of a verbalistic enthusiasm.'[21] Donald Gee says the same thing more simply and arrestingly: 'All Word and no Spirit — we dry up; all Spirit and no Word — we blow up; Word and

Spirit — we grow up.' Church history has repeatedly shown that, where there has been both a powerful and a continuous renewal of the Spirit, spilling over into effective evangelism, there has also been a firm stress on the truth of God's word, particularly in the preaching and teaching ministry, and in the growth of small house-groups. 'Virtually every major movement of spiritual renewal in the Christian Church has been accompanied by a return to the small group and the proliferation of such groups in private homes for Bible study, prayer, and the discussion of the faith.'[22] Conversely a tragic number of genuine movements of the Spirit have suddenly disappeared, or gone sour, or become heretical, owing to a neglect of the truth of God's word. The *Paraclete* passages in John, Chapters 14-16, make it clear that the Spirit who was coming to be with the disciples, to bear witness to Christ and to convict the world of sin, would do so by being the Spirit of truth. It is impossible to separate the teaching and witnessing aspects of the Spirit's work.

However, when the apostle John writes about the 'truth' he has in mind not so much propositional statements of theology as the *reality* of the person of Jesus Christ himself. Jesus said, 'I am the truth.'[23] Grace and truth came through Jesus Christ.[24] Therefore Jesus speaks the truth and bears witness to the truth.[25] Thus the truth that John talks about is the timeless reality of Christ, and this truth brings life to all who receive it. The Spirit of truth is also, therefore, the Spirit of life, and unless the Spirit is active in communicating that life a man cannot see and cannot enter the Kingdom of God.[26] We have already seen in chapter 3 that God communicates himself to us in a whole variety of ways, and although considerable stress must always be placed on the public and private ministry of teaching, the Church must become a witnessing community, controlled and empowered by the Spirit of God, before the reality of Christ can be *seen* as well as heard. It is no doubt for this reason that in the Epistles there is scarcely any reference to the power of the Spirit for the witnessing Church. Instead, the Holy Spirit is the distributor of various gifts to the Church,[27] the guarantee of our inheritance,[28] the means of access to the Father,[29] the bringer of God's love to our hearts,[30] the means of sanctification,[31] the ground of unity,[32] and the producer of love, joy, peace, patience, kindness, goodness, faithfulness, gentleness and self-control.[33] Here the emphasis on the Spirit's work has moved away from power in preaching the gospel, to a growing manifestation of the life of the risen Christ in local churches, without which all preaching would soon degenerate into a babble of words, 'full of sound and fury, signifying nothing'.

4. *The Holy Spirit and Conversion.* Any book on evangelism will of necessity stress in large measure what *we* must do as God's agents in the world. It is up to us to preach the gospel and to be relevant in today's society, and even the word 'conversion' speaks primarily of man's action: *we* must turn to Christ and help others to turn to Christ. The task that John the Baptist was given was to 'turn many...to the Lord'.[34] Jesus warned us that 'unless you turn and become like children, you will never enter the kingdom of heaven'.[35] Paul was sent by Christ to the Gentiles 'that they may turn from darkness to light and from the power of Satan to God'.[36] In every New Testament reference, 'to convert' or 'to turn' is something that we must do; it is man's responsibility. Possibly for this reason, evangelism in this technological age is so often presented as a technique: follow these rules if you want to see results. We talk of evangelistic programmes and conversational formulas by which you can lead almost anyone to Christ within ten minutes. Dr. Jim Packer once highlighted this modern trend in an article on revival:

> Revival cannot be organized or planned by man. I once saw in an American journal an advertisement which began, in large letters, 'DON'T PLAN A REVIVAL' — and I thought, how remarkably right minded! But alas, the advertisement went on, in smaller type — 'until you have these FREE SAMPLES of Color Advertising planned especially for the Church which wants something different but must operate on a conservative budget'.[37]

In sharp contrast to the proud self-confidence of modern man in this machine age, the first Christians knew that without the Spirit's power they could not begin to turn man from darkness to God's marvellous light. They went in humble dependence on the Spirit, who alone could open the eyes of the spiritually blind and unstop deaf ears and warm cold hearts and bend proud wills. Unless the Spirit brought life, men and women were 'dead through the trespasses and sins'.[38] Unless there was a clear demonstration of the Spirit and power, the faith of those who believed would rest only in the wisdom of men and not in the power of God.[39] This would spell disaster for any true work for God that they were hoping to see.

In his book *Christian Mission in the Modern World*,[40] John Stott is careful, however, to explain what a right dependence on the Holy Spirit does *not* mean in the context of evangelism. First, it does not mean that there is no need to prepare before preaching. It is true that Jesus promised his disciples 'a mouth and wisdom' so that they did not need 'to meditate beforehand' how to speak, but he was referring specifically to being brought into court in the hour of persecution.[41] The promise has nothing whatever to do with preaching from a pulpit. Indeed, my common experience is that, when I hear someone claim that he always preaches 'spontaneously as the Spirit leads', I nearly always wish that he had taken the time and trouble to ask for the Spirit's guidance in careful preparation beforehand. Very likely the same basic material would have been preached in half the time and with twice the clarity.

Secondly, dependence on the Holy Spirit does not mean being anti-intellectual. When Paul said that he came to Corinth not 'in lofty words or wisdom' but in the power of the Spirit, he was not disparaging a true intellectual content in his gospel preaching: his mind-stimulating Epistles should make that obvious. Often he sought to 'persuade' men of the truth of the gospel, and no doubt there was some solid reasoning involved in that persuasion. Instead, he was refusing to employ the rhetorical tricks and flamboyant eloquence of the Greek debaters when it came to the eternal truths of Jesus Christ and him crucified. It was in this seemingly foolish message that God had invested his power.

Thirdly, relying on the Holy Spirit does not mean being irrelevant. The impression is sometimes given that, providing the Spirit is at work in answer to believing prayer, then almost any word, any translation of the Bible and any presentation of the message will do. Communication is inevitable when the Spirit is there. Of course, the Spirit *has* sometimes taken the most clumsy sermon and the most out-dated presentation, and brought people to Christ with tremendous power. In his sovereignty there is no situation that he cannot use. And, on the other hand, the most contemporary proclamation of the gospel will seem cheap and gimmicky without the Spirit's presence. But there is no excuse for laziness. Christians need to follow the example of Paul and the other apostles in seeking to make the gospel utterly relevant in the society in which they live and work. What does it communicate today? How can the minds and hearts of people be reached in an age which is so ignorant of the gospel and so far removed from the Church? Fourthly, trusting the Holy Spirit does not mean suppressing our human personality. The desire to be 'hidden' in order that Christ may be seen can lead to colourless Christian lives which will hardly commend the Author of life or the abundant life that he promises to bring. The biblical record is that God has always worked through human personality, created, fashioned and inspired by his Spirit. See the strong and varied personalities of the apostles or prophets. See Moses striding down Mount Sinai to smash the golden calf to bits, and yet he was known as 'the meekest man on the face of the earth'. See Peter at Pentecost, or Paul on Mars Hill, or Philip at Samaria, or Stephen before the council. As John Stott rightly concludes his book:

> What Scripture lays upon us is the need for a proper combination of humility and humanity — the humility to let God be God, acknowledging that he alone can give sight to the blind and life to the dead, and the humanity to be ourselves as he has made us, not suppressing our personal individuality, but exercising our God-given gifts and offering ourselves to God as instruments of righteousness in his hand. I wonder if anything is more needed for the Christian mission in the modern age than this healthy fusion of humility and humanity in our reliance on the power of the Holy Spirit.[42]

Further, the Holy Spirit is not only indispensable in the work of conversion; he is also very much a part of the message of the gospel. When the crowd asked Peter, 'What shall we do?' he told them to repent and be baptised in the name of Jesus Christ, 'and you shall receive the gift of the Holy Spirit'.[43] In Samaria it was not enough for the people to receive the word of God and to be baptised; Peter and John prayed specifically for them that they might receive the Holy Spirit.[44] Ananias explained to Saul of Tarsus that he had been sent by God to him 'that you may regain your sight and be filled with the Holy Spirit'.[45] When Paul met some disciples at Ephesus his first question to them was, 'Did you receive the Holy Spirit when you believed?' Although there should be no rigid formula, it is both wise and biblical to say something about the person of the Holy Spirit at the time of conversion. Some of the best-known evangelistic booklets have not a single reference to the Spirit; and this no doubt contributes to the confusion surrounding the Spirit's work at the time of, and subsequent to, conversion.

5. *The Holy Spirit and Guidance.* Evangelism is often hindered in the Church today, not through the laziness of Christians, but through the busyness of Christians in the wrong directions. Many ministers I know are tired, hard-pressed and overworked, with sometimes not very much to show for all their labours. However, it was a marked feature of the first-century Church that it moved and acted under the guidance of the Holy Spirit. What can we learn from its example? First, guidance is usually *natural.* When Paul came to Thessalonica he went straight to the synagogue, *'as was his custom,* and for three weeks he argued with them from the Scriptures' about Jesus Christ.[46] In the absence of clear and specific guidance to the contrary, Paul went to the obvious place where he would meet those who believed in God. There was a considerable response to the gospel, especially from some godly Greeks, but also from some of the Jews. On an earlier occasion, Peter and John were used by God to bring healing to a cripple, resulting in the conversion of some two thousand, and all this happened when they were 'going up to the temple at the hour of prayer', which was doubtless their

daily practice.[47] In other words, God wants us to use our minds and common sense, because guidance is usually thoroughly rational. In trusting in the Holy Spirit we must beware of a super-spirituality which is always looking for the unusual in God's guidance.

Secondly, guidance is often *corporate*; it is not a private affair. Even after Paul and Peter had various visions and revelations, making it clear to them that the gospel was for the Gentiles as well as for the Jews, they still submitted this revolutionary idea to the leaders of the church at Jerusalem. There was a considerable debate, and they listened carefully to Peter, Paul and Barnabas 'as they related what signs and wonders God had done through them among the Gentiles'. Eventually they sent their conclusion to the church at Antioch, explaining that 'it has seemed good to the Holy Spirit and to us'.[48] This was a thoroughly democratic discussion and decision. No doubt they prayed together about the whole affair (although Luke does not specifically mention this); yet at the end of the day they felt confident that their corporate conclusion was also the guidance of the Holy Spirit.

Thirdly, guidance is sometimes *special*. It was clearly so with Philip when the angel led him into the Gaza desert to seek out the Ethiopian Chancellor of the Exchequer who was hungry for God, and when the Spirit of the Lord took Philip away at the right time, leaving the Chancellor rejoicing in Christ.[49] God also gave special guidance to Ananias, speaking through a vision, and giving him gifts of knowledge, wisdom, prophecy, faith and healing, in order to be God's messenger to Saul.[50] Again God's Spirit guided with visions and other spiritual gifts in order to bring Peter into the house of Cornelius, the Gentile.[51] In both these cases, God had to overcome the deep-rooted prejudices that Ananias had towards Saul, and that Peter had towards the Gentiles; therefore some unusual features in their guidance were only to be expected. In Acts, Chapter 13, prophetic guidance came to the prophets and teachers at Antioch concerning their next missionary advance after a time of worshipping the Lord and fasting. In Acts, Chapter 16, Paul and his companions found the matter of guidance frankly a puzzling business. They were 'forbidden by the Holy Spirit to speak the word in

Asia' (Luke does not record whether it was a vision, prophecy or circumstances which prevented them from going there); later 'the Spirit of Jesus did not allow them' to go into Bithynia; but Paul then had a vision in the night calling them to Macedonia. 'Immediately,' writes Luke, 'we sought to go on into Macedonia, concluding that God had called us to preach the gospel to them.'[52] However, it had been a somewhat frustrating and puzzling time, as guidance often is.

Nevertheless without some understanding of the will and plan of the Lord, so much of our work and evangelism can be little more than 'beating the air'. When my wife and I moved to York in 1965, we were faced with an all but redundant church, a tiny congregation, no money, a large, damp and filthy Victorian house to live in, and we had really no idea of what we should do and where we should start. Certainly we began in an obvious and natural way, knocking on doors in the parish, and no doubt that had its place. But after some time of considerable frustration the two of us agreed to set aside the best part of one day a week for prayer and fasting to try to discover where God was leading us and what he was wanting us to do. In the first week after we began, we saw four people commit their lives to Christ, and in our first year almost all our fruitful steps forward came as a result of those days of prayer. I often think of that startling catch of fish by Simon Peter, in obedience to Christ's will, after a whole night of fruitless fishing, and of the simple lesson that he learnt (and he had to learn it again and again): that knowing God's will and obeying it is worth infinitely more than endlessly toiling away in our own strength. It is the desire of the Holy Spirit to make known to us the will of God, and then to give us the strength to do it.

6. *The Holy Spirit and Prayer.* Dr. J. I. Packer wrote that, 'where we are not consciously relying on God, there we shall inevitably be found relying on ourselves. And the spirit of self-reliance is a blight on evangelism.'[53] A conscious reliance upon God, in specific terms, involves one essential ingredient: much prayer. One of the most crucial lessons to grasp in evangelism is that we are engaged in a powerful spiritual warfare. Behind the apathy which Paul found so hard to overcome in his day (as most of us do today), there is the god

of this world blinding the minds of unbelievers so that they cannot see the light of the gospel of the glory of Christ.[54] Therefore whether we realise it or not, we are battling with unseen Satanic forces as we urge people to turn from darkness to light and from the power of Satan to God. Nowhere does Paul speak so clearly about this as in Ephesians, Chapter 6, where he stresses the need to be strong in the Lord and to put on the whole armour of God, 'for we are not contending against flesh and blood, but against the principalities, against the powers, against the world rulers of this present darkness, against the spiritual hosts of wickedness in the heavenly places'. Then, having exhorted the Ephesian church to put on the gospel armour piece by piece, he tells them to 'pray at all times in the Spirit, with all prayer and supplication'. He particularly asks them to pray for him 'that utterance may be given me in opening my mouth boldly to proclaim the mystery of the gospel'. Paul knew the absolute folly of trying to proclaim the gospel without Spirit-inspired prayer. How can we expect to see miracles of new birth taking place without much prayer, and possibly fasting as well? How can we ever see men and women brought out of Satan's kingdom into God's Kingdom, unless we humbly acknowledge our own utter weakness and call upon God for his strength? Writing to the Corinthians, Paul reminds them that 'we are not carrying on a worldly war, for the weapons of our warfare are not worldly but have divine power to destroy strongholds. We destroy arguments and every proud obstacle to the knowledge of God, and take every thought captive to obey Christ.'[55] And from Ephesians, Chapter 6, the main weapons that Paul discovered had 'divine power to destroy strongholds' were the weapons of 'the sword of the Spirit, which is the word of God', and prayer.

In virtually every evangelistic activity I have ever taken part in, I have sooner or later been forcibly reminded of the spiritual battle, if I have not given it due consideration from the start. Frequently God has brought us to our knees in more fervent and urgent prayer half-way through a mission because nothing seems to be happening. Sometimes there have been specific attacks on the home during evangelistic work. Over the course of a year or more I became increasingly aware of the fact that our special guest services were almost always accompanied by domestic disturbances or sickness. Then, when this had been made a matter for specific prayer, many of these disruptions ceased. Certainly there will be battles, but we need to understand that these will be essentially spiritual conflicts, and God has given us the information and resources we need to resist the devil until he flees from us. When the seventy reported back to Jesus, jubilant as they were after a thrilling mission when they had seen 'even demons' subject to them in Christ's name, Jesus replied, 'I saw Satan fall like lightning from heaven. Behold, I have given you authority to tread upon serpents and scorpions, and over all the power of the enemy.'[56]

Clearly the one factor above all others which released the disciples into spontaneous evangelism, which made them effective with the sword of the Spirit, and which enabled them to pray in the Spirit, was the filling of the Holy Spirit of God. When Christians are truly and continuously filled with the Spirit there is no limit to what God can do amongst them. Duncan Campbell once said that the Kingdom of God would be advanced, not by churches filled with people, but by people filled with the Holy Spirit, and therefore this was the greatest need of the day. Undoubtedly this was the factor which empowered the evangelists of a previous generation. D. L. Moody wrote, 'One day in the city of New York, oh what a day, I cannot describe it, it is almost too sacred an experience to name. I can only say that God revealed himself to me and I had such an experience of his love that I had to ask him to stay his hand.' R. A. Torrey, Charles G. Finney, and A. T. Pierson spoke of similar experiences which equipped them for fruitful evangelism. Jonathan Edwards, the American revivalist of the eighteenth century, defied virtually every rule of 'dynamic' preaching. He wrote down almost every word of his sermons, and, as he was short-sighted, he would stand in the pulpit with sermon notes in one hand and a candle in the other. Yet as he read his sermons, peering at his script, not only were many converted but also some fell to the ground because of the extraordinary power of the Spirit that was released.

Today, God is bringing similar blessings to large numbers

of Christians throughout the world. The terminology differs, and there is in some circles a need for a much clearer biblical understanding of the experience of spiritual renewal. But the reality is there. One C.M.S. missionary wrote about 'release from bondage, new freedom to love, deep welling joy and a song of praise: this is what baptism in the Spirit has meant to me, an unbelievably gracious gift of God'. Sadly, not all claims to being filled with the Spirit have led to an increase in evangelism, and there have been many confusing counterfeits of the real thing. However, it may be God's purpose for today not necessarily to raise up a Moody, Torrey or Finney as outstanding individual evangelists, but to renew congregations and to bring to life local churches where all the gifts and ministries will come into their own, only one of these gifts being specifically that of evangelist. Here it is the whole body of Christians that, when empowered by the Spirit of God, will most effectively communicate Christ. We need to remember, too, that in Acts, Chapters 2, and 4, the Spirit filled all the disciples together. And when Paul wrote, 'Be filled with the Spirit',[57] he was addressing himself to the whole Ephesian church, not primarily to one or two special Christians. It is our corporate control by the Holy Spirit that we need, more than anything else, in evangelism.

How can we be filled with the Spirit and equipped with the power of God to accomplish his work? First we must *repent* of all known sin, because being filled with the Spirit means asking the Holy Spirit of God to control every area of our lives, and we cannot ask for that sincerely if we are not willing to release some area of our life into his hands. It will be necessary, therefore, to let the Spirit examine our hearts in order to reveal to us any aspects of our lives which need to be dealt with before we go any further. Certainly we cannot make ourselves holy; but we can, and must, repent specifically of anything which may grieve the Spirit and prevent him from filling our lives with the love and power of God. Some may find it helpful to work prayerfully through a list of searching questions. John Wesley, and many others whom God has used, knew the great importance of this. In his book *Blessings out of Buffetings* Alan Redpath records that he uses these questions 'at least once a week, and often every day':

Am I consciously or unconsciously creating the impression that I am a better man than I really am? In other words, am I a hypocrite?

Am I honest in all my acts or words, or do I exaggerate?

Do I confidentially pass on to another what was told to me in confidence?

Can I be trusted?

Am I a slave to dress, friends, work or habits?

Am I self-conscious, self-pitying or self-justifying?

Did the Bible live to me today?

Do I give it time to speak to me every day?

Am I enjoying prayer?

When did I last speak to somebody else with the object of trying to win that person for Christ?

Am I making contacts with other people and using them for the Master's glory?

Do I pray about the money I spend?

Do I get to bed in time and get up in time?

Do I disobey God in anything?

Do I insist upon doing something about which my conscience is uneasy?

Am I defeated in any part of my life, jealous, impure, critical, irritable, touchy or distrustful?

How do I spend my spare time?

Am I proud?

Do I thank God that I am not as other people, especially as the Pharisee who despised the publican?

Is there anybody whom I fear, dislike, disown, criticize, hold a resentment toward or disregard? If so, what am I doing about it?

Do I grumble or complain constantly?

Is Christ real to me?[58]

There may well be other questions that we could helpfully add to this, concerning our loving service and commitment towards one another, and our willingness to be used by God in whatever way he chooses, submitting to one another out of reverence to Christ. If, however, having prayed over a list like this, we feel that we have 0 out of 100, it does not mean that we are disqualified from being filled with the Spirit; for who can begin to deserve any of God's gifts? Rather, the Holy Spirit may use such questions to show us our need and failure, and then bring us to the point of repentance. If we are not willing to repent, this may take some time. But *as soon as* we have consciously repented of every known sin, we have taken the first vital step towards being filled by the Spirit.

Secondly, we must be willing to *obey* God wherever he may lead us. When the Spirit came upon the disciples at Pentecost, it was not the beginning of a glory-trip for them, with all their problems disappearing overnight. In one sense their problems had only just begun. Soon they were imprisoned, beaten, persecuted, scattered from their homes, stoned, shipwrecked, cold, hungry, thirsty, exhausted, in constant danger, and with numerous pressures and anxieties weighing upon them.[59] Paul wrote about being 'afflicted...perplexed-...struck down...always carrying in the body the death of Jesus'.[60] *This* is what being filled with the Spirit meant to them, but because they were willing to obey God, whatever price they had to pay, his power was manifestly amongst them. In a thought-provoking passage, A. W. Tozer once wrote:

Are you sure that you want to be possessed by a Spirit who, while he is pure and gentle and wise, will insist upon being Lord of your life? Are you sure you want your personality to be taken over by One who will require obedience to the written word? Who will not tolerate any of the self-sins in your life: self-love, self-indulgence? Who will not permit you to boast or strut or show off? Who will take the direction of your life away from you and will reserve the sovereign right to test you and discipline you? Unless you can answer an eager 'Yes' to these questions, you do not want to be filled. You want the thrill or the victory or the power, but you do not really want to be filled with the Spirit.

Thirdly, we must be *hungry and thirsty* for the Lord and for a life of righteousness in his sight. It is when we long that God should be glorified in our lives and are distressed by our

emptiness and powerlessness, that we can ask to be filled by
him. It is when we desire, above all, that God should be
honoured as God, worshipped and adored, loved and served,
not only by ourselves but also by others around us, including
those who as yet do not know him at all — it is then that we
are ready to be filled. We may feel our faith and general
spiritual condition to be weak, but then a man who is really
hungry and thirsty will hardly feel strong and healthy.
Nevertheless, Jesus always comes to us most graciously when
we are most conscious of our absolute need of him; and to
those in this condition he says, 'If any one thirst, let him come
to me and drink. He who believes in me, as the Scripture has
said, "Out of his heart shall flow rivers of living water."'[61]
Quite simply, then, we must come and *drink*: that is, ask for,
and by faith receive, the gift that God is always longing to
give us, when our hearts are made clean by the blood of Jesus
and wide open to his love. Further, in that invitation all the
verbs are in the present tense, which means that the filling of
the Spirit is never a package-deal. Instead, we must go on
being thirsty, since we can never claim to have arrived. We
are never more than 'earthen vessels', although at best these
earthen vessels of ours can be filled with God's transcendent
power. Thus we must go on coming to Jesus, and go on
drinking from him; only then will those rivers of living water
go on flowing from our innermost being.

Christ today is reigning in heaven. One day, at the name of
Jesus every knee shall bow and every tongue shall confess that
Jesus Christ is Lord. Until that glorious and awesome day, he
has both commissioned us with the task of proclaiming him to
the world as Lord and Saviour, and equipped us with all that
we need to accomplish that task. 'This Jesus God raised up, and
of that we all are witnesses. Being therefore exalted at the right
hand of God, and having received from the Father the promise
of the Holy Spirit, he has poured out this which you see and
hear.'[62] So Peter was able to preach on the day of Pentecost. It is
this same Spirit of the living God that needs to fall afresh on us
today, if our belief in evangelism is to bear fruit. God has not
withdrawn his gift or his promise. He waits for us, his children,
to come to him with all our obvious need; and he will then give
the Holy Spirit to those who ask him.

NOTES

1   Ephesians 2:20, p. 168.
2   Acts 5:12-16, p. 168.
3   Acts 19:11f, p. 169.
4   John 15:26f, p. 169.
5   John 16:7f, p. 169.
6   Acts 1:8, p. 169.
7   H. Boer, *Pentecost and Missions* (Lutterworth, 1961),
    122, 128, p. 169.
8   Acts 5:28, p. 170.
9   Luke 24:46-9, p. 171.
10 Acts 4:31, 33, p. 171.
11 1 Corinthians 2:3-5, p. 171.
12 1 Thessalonians 1:5, p. 172.
13 Luke 11:13, p. 172.
14 Luke 4:1, 14, p. 172.
15 Acts 5:27-42, p. 172.
16 Acts 6:7, p. 172.
17 Acts 6:8ff, p. 173.
18 Ephesians 5:18, 21, p. 173.
19 Acts 4:24-33, p. 173.
20 John 15:26; 16:13, p. 173.
21 Hans Küng, *The Church* (Search Press, 1968) 202f, p. 173.
22 H. Snyder in *Let the Earth Hear His Voice,* 340, p. 174.
23 John 14:6, p. 174.
24 John 1:17, p. 174.
25 John 8:40, 45; 18:37, p. 174.
26 John 3:3-7, p. 174.
27 1 Corinthians 12; Hebrews 2:4, p. 174.
28 Ephesians 1:14, p. 174.
29 Ephesians 2:18, p. 174.
30 Romans 5:5, p. 174.
31 1 Peter 1:2, p. 174.
32 Ephesians 4:3, p. 174.
33 Galatians 5:22f, p. 175.
34 Luke 1:16, p. 175.
35 Matthew 18:3, p. 175.
36 Acts 26:18; cf. 9:35; 11:21; 26:20, p. 175.
37 *The Christian Graduate,* December 1971, p. 175.
38 Ephesians 2:1, p. 176.
39 1 Corinthians 2:4f, p. 176.
40 (Falcon), 1975, p. 176.
41 Luke 21:12-15, p. 176.
42 Op. cit., 128, p. 177.
43 Acts 2:38, p. 178.

44   Acts 8:14-17, p. 178.
45   Acts 9:17, p. 178.
46   Acts 17:2, p. 178.
47   Acts 3:1-10, p. 179.
48   Acts 15, p. 179.
49   Acts 8:26-39, p. 179.
50   Acts 9:10-19, p. 179.
51   Acts 10-11, p. 179.
52   Acts 16:6-10, p. 180.
53   *Evangelism and the Sovereignty of God* (I.V.P.), 29, p. 180.
54   2 Corinthians 4:4, p. 181.
55   2 Corinthians 10:3-5, p. 181.
56   Luke 10:18f, p. 182.
57   Ephesians 5:18, p. 183.
58   Op. cit. (Pickering & Inglis), 235f, p. 183.
59   See 2 Corinthians 11:23-9, p. 185.
60   2 Corinthians 4:7-12, p. 185.
61   John 7:37f, p. 186.
62   Acts 2:32f, p. 186.

APPENDIX

Here is a list of passages which may prove of value for Bible
Study on certain subjects:

General

Psalm 27	Psalm 34	Psalm 37:1-13
Psalm 62	Psalm 63	Psalm 103
Joshua 1:1-9	Luke 24:13-32	John 10
John 15	I Thessalonians 5:14-25	

Sin

Psalm 32	Psalm 51	Psalm 139:1-14, 23-4
Isaiah 6:1-8	Luke 15:11-24	Luke 18:9-23

The Cross

Psalm 22:1-18	Psalm 116	Isaiah 53
Matthew 27:39-51	Romans 3:20-8	Romans 5:1-11

The Cost

2 Kings 5:1-14	Luke 9:57-62	Luke 14:25-33
Philippians 3:1-14	Revelation 3:13-22	

The Gospel

Psalm 34:1-10	Psalm 40	Isaiah 55:1-11
Luke 15:1-10	Luke 18:35-43	Luke 19:1-10
John 3:1-17	John 3:9-21	Acts 8:26-39
Acts 9:1-18	Ephesians 2:1-14	

Assurance

Psalm 103	Psalm 116	Psalm 121
Psalm 124	Romans 5:1-11	Romans 8:28-39
I Thessalonians 1	I Peter 1:3-9	

Temptation

Ephesians 6:10-20   James 1:1-15

Growth

Psalm 84   Philippians 3:7-16   2 Timothy 2:1-12

Trusting and Victory

Psalm 16   Matthew 4:1-11   Matthew 8:1-13
Matthew 14:22-33   John 15:1-14   Romans 6:11-23
Philippians 4:4-19 Hebrews 11:32-12:2 1 John 1

Prayer

1 Chronicles
29:10-19   Isaiah 64:1-18   Luke 11:1-13
John 17:6-17   Ephesians 1:15-23   Ephesians 3:14-21
Colossians 1:9-14 Philippians 4:4-19

Witness and Service

Matthew 5:1-16   Mark 2:1-12   John 4:1-26
John 6:1-15   John 21:15-end   Acts 3:1-11
Acts 8:26-40   Romans 12:1-15   I Corinthians 13
2 Corinthians 4:1-10 2 Corinthians
                   5:10-21   Ephesians 5:8-21
I Peter 3:8-18   I Peter 5:1-11

The Bible

Psalm 1   Psalm 119 (various
                              sections)

Guidance

Proverbs 3:1-12